Rose Rosenau

THE WOLF
WITHIN

THE WOLF WITHIN

A New Approach to Caring for your Dog

David Alderton

HOWELL BOOK HOUSE
NEW YORK

CONTENTS

First published by Howell Book House
A Simon & Schuster Macmillan Company
1633 Broadway
New York, NY 10019

MACMILLAN is a registered trademark of
Macmillan, Inc.

**Library of Congress Cataloging-in-
Publication Data**
A catalog record for this book is available
from the Library of Congress

ISBN 0-87605-612-5

This book was designed and produced by
Quarto Publishing plc
The Old Brewery
6 Blundell Street
LONDON
N7 9BH

Senior Editor: Gerrie Purcell
Copy editor: Eleanor Van Zandt
Art Editor/Designer: Julie Francis
Photographers: Bruce Tanner, Les Wies
Illustrators: Robert Morton, Janice
Nicolson
Picture Research: Zoë Holtermann
Editorial Director: Pippa Rubinstein
Art Director: Moira Clinch

Typeset by: Central Southern
Typesetters,
Eastbourne, Great
Britain
Manufactured by:
Universal Graphics Pte
Ltd, Singapore
Printed by:
Star Standard
Industries (Pte) Ltd,
Singapore

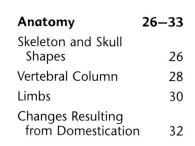

DOGS:

FROM

THE WILD

The domestic dog still displays many of the behavioral traits of its ancestor, the grey wolf, in spite of a domestication process that occurred over many thousands of years. It is ironic that since dogs have become popular as household companions as well as working animals, the grey wolf itself has been eliminated from much of its former range by human persecution. The adaptability of wild canids is aptly demonstrated by the red fox, which is now commonly found living in cities, not just in the northern hemisphere, but also in Australia, where it has been introduced.

WILD COUSINS

Although, in some cases, the appearance of the domestic dog has diverged significantly from that of its ancestor, the grey wolf, all dogs still retain many features — both anatomical and behavioral — in common with their wild relatives. There are thirty-three different species grouped in their family, Canidae, ranging from the far north down to the tip of South America. The only inhabited continent without a native population of wild dogs is Australia. The red fox was introduced there in the mid-eighteenth century, while the dingo was brought to Australia by early human settlers.

Arctic fox (*Alopex lagopus*)
Circumpolar
Ranging over the frozen north, the Arctic fox wanders from the former Soviet Union to Alaska. It is well adapted to survive in this terrain, with hair on the soles of its feet as protection against frostbite. Its ears are small for the same reason, while its coat is thick, providing insulation against the cold. There are two different color forms of the Arctic fox. Some are pure white, whereas others have blue fur with a grayish tinge. In summer these two forms become brownish and a dark chocolate shade respectively, which gives better camouflage. Rodents, especially lemmings, feature in their diet, but Arctic foxes will scavenge and even eat berries.

Coyote (*Canis latrans*)
North and Central America
There is a wide range in size among these wild dogs. Coyotes from northern areas, weighing up to 75lb (34kg), may be three times heavier than those at the southern end of their range, in Mexico. Its name comes from the Aztec word *coyotl*, meaning "barking dog." Smaller and more adaptable than wolves, the coyote has expanded its range from the western plains of North America as the wolf population has declined, in spite of heavy persecution from farmers. The coyote feeds on rabbits, carrion and rodents, as well as on lambs and goats.

Grey wolf (*Canis lupus*)
North America, Europe and Asia
The largest member of the family, the grey wolf used to range across most of the northern hemisphere. Today its distribution has been greatly reduced by human persecution and increasing urbanization. Living in packs, this wolf needs large areas where it can hunt prey such as deer. Recently, more enlightened attitudes have led to this wolf being successfully reintroduced to areas where it had been eliminated.

Red wolf (*Canis rufus*)
North America
Saved from extinction by a captive breeding program, the future of the red wolf is still uncertain. It used to occur widely through the southeastern United States, from central Texas to Florida. Loss of habitat and hunting pressures added to its decline. The first captive-bred red wolves were released into the wild in 1988, eight years after the species had vanished, and some have bred successfully there. Hybridization with the coyote, which has colonized the former territory of the red wolf, remains an on-going threat.

New World Canids

The majority of wild canids are found in the Americas, but there is a clear split in their distribution here. The range of those found in the north, such as the coyote, does not extend into South America. Smaller foxes predominate on the southern continent. They are often described as zorros.

1 Red wolf
2 Coyote
3 Maned wolf
4 Grey fox
5 Swift fox
6 Culpeo
7 Grey Zorro

8 Crab-eating Zorro
9 Small-eared Zorro
10 Island grey fox
11 Hoary Zorro
12 Bush dog
13 Sechuran zorro
14 Azara's zorro

Grey fox (*Urocyon cinereoargenteus*)
North, Central and South America
Also known as the tree-climbing fox, this species, with its short legs, is an agile climber, unlike other wild dogs. The dens of the grey fox can be located in trees as high as 9m (30ft), although this fox may prefer to live underground, especially in the northern part of its range, which extends up to the Canadian border. Its diet varies from small mammals and birds to invertebrates and fruit. Young are born with black coats.

Island grey fox (*Urocyon littoralis*)
North America
This fox is confined to six of the eight Channel Islands found off the coast of southern California.

Similar in appearance to the grey fox, it is descended from the same ancestral stock. The island grey fox is smaller than its mainland relative and distinguishable by a shorter tail.

Swift fox (*Vulpes velox*)
North America
Occurring in the western areas of the United States, the swift fox has been recently reintroduced in Canada, where it had become extinct. Poisoned baits left for coyotes have been a major cause in its decline. Coyotes will also kill this fox, making it vulnerable in areas where coyote numbers remain largely unchecked.

Red fox (*Vulpes vulpes*)
North America, Europe, Africa and Asia
More adaptable than the grey wolf, the red fox has spread

over a wider area in recent years. It is now a common sight in cities, where it has adapted to living, scavenging in garbage bags and on the streets for food, as well as hunting birds and rodents. Its distribution in Africa is presently restricted to northern areas. Red foxes taken from Europe to Australia for fox-hunting from 1845 onward have now overrun that continent. There they benefitted from the introduction of rabbits.

Golden jackal (*Canis aureus*)
Africa, Europe and Asia
This jackal occurs right across northern Africa and the Middle East, with its Asiatic range currently extending eastward to Thailand. Its range also extends further north than that of other jackals, into southeastern parts of Europe. It has a reputation

African Canids

While the majority of the African species are solitary by nature, the African wild dog lives in packs. It is therefore a formidable hunter, compared with most other canids which depend on smaller quarry such as rodents as a major part of their diet.

1 Black-backed jackal
2 African hunting dog
3 Cape fox
4 Side-striped jackal
5 Pale fox
6 Ethiopian jackal
7 Bat-eared fox
8 Fennec fox

for scavenging, but will also hunt, depending on the availability of prey. In Israel, snakes are hunted, as was shown after a poisoning campaign led to a decline in the number of jackals but an increase in snakebites among the people in these areas.

Side-striped jackal (*Canis adustus*)
Africa
This species occurs in the tropical areas of Africa, typically in forested areas. It has distinctive lines of pale hairs running down each side of its body, and a stronger, more powerful muzzle than other jackals. In agricultural areas it often steals vegetables, as well as feeding on carrion and rodents. This jackal is hunted in some areas for its body parts — the skin and claws are reputed to ward off evil spirits.

Black-backed jackal (*Canis mesomelas*)
Africa
There are two widely separated populations of this jackal. The southern group ranges across Africa from Angola and Zimbabwe to the Cape, while the northern distribution is centered on East Africa. This species is also known as the silver-backed jackal, because of the coloration on its back. The young are grayish in color at first, only acquiring their adult coloration after three months.

Ethiopian jackal (*Canis simensis*)
Africa
Known for a period as the Simien fox, this very rare species is mainly confined to the Balé Mountains National Park in Ethiopia. Current population estimates suggest there are around 700 of these jackals living there. Unlike most wild dogs, it often proves quite tame, remaining as close as 10ft (3m) to people, making it very vulnerable to hunters.

African hunting dog (*Lycaon pictus*)
Africa
The distribution of this species is greatly reduced, for reasons similar to those underlying the decline of the grey wolf. Both live in packs and hunt large prey, including wildebeest in the case of the African hunting dog. The size of the pack has also fallen — today, groups of more than thirty are rare, while formerly, groups of a hundred or more were quite common. A feature of African hunting dog packs is that they comprise predominantly of related males.

Cape fox (*Vulpes chama*)
Africa
Confined to the southern part of the African continent, as far north as the Zambezi River, this is the only *Vulpes* species found south of the equator. The Cape fox inhabits fairly open areas of country and usually hides during the day. It frequents arid areas and hunts a variety of small prey, as well as feeding on plants and berries. Solitary by nature, this fox also scavenges on human refuse and has been blamed for killing lambs, although it is more likely to feed on dead carcasses.

Fennec fox (*Fennecus zerda*)
Africa
This species is the smallest of all the wild dogs, being roughly the size of a small lapdog and weighing just 2–3lb (1–1.5kg). Large ears help the fennec fox locate its prey, which, in the deserts of northern Africa where it lives, consists mainly of rodents. But this fox can also kill creatures larger than itself, such as rabbits. The fennec fox lives in an underground den, where it retreats in the heat. It communicates not only by barking, but also, within the family group, by a sound similar to purring.

Pale fox (*Vulpes pallida*)
Africa
Also known as the African sand fox, this species is found in a broad band across northern Africa, in the Sahel region bordering the Sahara Desert. It is heavier than the fennec fox, weighing as much as 6lb (3kg) and measuring 10in (25cm) at the shoulder. Coloration varies from pale red to sandy buff.

Rüppell's fox (*Vulpes rueppelli*)
Africa, Middle East and Asia
This fox occurs further north than the pale fox, from Morocco across the Arabian peninsula to Afghanistan and Pakistan. They are similar in size, but Rüppell's fox has larger ears, while its coloration may range from buff to a more grayish shade.

Blanford's fox (*Vulpes cana*)
Middle East and Asia
Reports suggest the range of Blanford's fox is now greater than previously thought and may extend into parts of the Middle East, from its traditional areas in Afghanistan and southwestern parts of the former Soviet Union. This fox has a slender snout, which suggests that insects and fruit may feature in its diet. It has been recorded eating fruit and may also hunt small rodents.

Bat-eared fox (*Otocyon megalotis*)
Africa
There are two distinctive populations of this fox, located in the eastern and southern parts of Africa. The bat-eared fox has large ears, up to 5 inches (13cm) long, with black tips, which has led to its also being known as the black-eared fox. It is primarily insectivorous, feeding on termites and beetles.

Bengal fox (*Vulpes bengalensis*)
Asia
This fox is widely distributed across the Indian subcontinent, being more common in open areas of countryside than woodland. Pairs appear to live together for most of the year, but may hunt separately. The Bengal fox lives in a den, which may take the form of either a simple tunnel or a complex network of interconnecting chambers with different exits above ground.

Corsac fox (*Vulpes corsac*)
Asia
Present in central Asia, with its distribution extending eastward to Mongolia, these foxes live at relatively high densities in some areas, occupying neighboring burrows, hence the description "corsac cities." Heavily hunted for its fur, it has become scarce in some areas. Plowing has also contributed to its decline, destroying traditional den sites.

Tibetan fox (*Vulpes ferrilata*)
Asia
Confined to Tibet and nearby areas, this fox occurs at high altitudes, where it often seeks shelter among piles of boulders, or burrows beneath large rocks. The Tibetan fox has a long snout and powerful teeth, which indicates it may feed mainly on rodents, but little is known about its habits. A dense coat, combined with small ears, helps to provide protection against the cold. This fox is trapped for its pelt, which is used to make hats.

Dhole (*Cuon alpinus*)
Asia
Remains of dholes confirm that groups used to be found in Europe. Today its distribution ranges eastward from India as far as China and south to Java. Dholes live in packs of a dozen or more individuals, many of which are related. Outside the breeding season, packs may form larger units of a hundred or more individuals, which are described as "clans." This wild dog hunts large prey, including deer. It communicates by means of howling whistles.

Maned wolf (*Chrysocyon brachyurus*)
South America
In spite of its name, this species is more closely related to foxes. The maned wolf may stand 29 inches (76cm) high at the shoulder. Its height enables it to see for a long way in the grassland areas it inhabits. Birds are a main part of its diet, with the wolf's speed and agility helping it to catch such quarry, which may include domestic chickens. Rodents are also eaten regularly, as well as fruit.

Culpeo (*Dusicyon culpaeus*)
South America
The range of this fox extends along the length of South America, adjoining the western seaboard. It is the largest member of the genus, with the biggest examples coming from the southern end of its distribution. It will take lambs, but the culpeo feeds mainly on rodents and rabbits.

Crab-eating zorro (*Cerdocyon thous*)
South America
The Spanish word *zorro* is used for many foxes from this continent, distinguishing them from the Old World *Vulpes* species. The crab-eating zorro has a wide range, being most common in the central area — in Bolivia, Paraguay, Uruguay and Argentina. It eats land crabs on occasions, but also takes other foods, even bananas.

Azara's zorro (*Dusicyon gymnocercus*)
South America
This species occurs in a wide range of habitats. It has a solitary lifestyle, preying on a range of small animals, as well as birds. Persecuted in some areas, it displays great fear of people, often reacting by freezing, in the hope of escaping detection.

Grey zorro (*Dusicyon griseus*)
South America
This species is mainly gray, and has suffered heavy persecution for its fur. The grey zorro is small, compared with other members of its genus, weighing little more than 9lb (4kg). It ranges down to the tip of the continent, where the weather can be bitter in winter.

Small-eared zorro (*Dusicyon microtis*)
South America
One of the most mysterious members of the genus, whose habits are largely unknown. The small-eared zorro lives in the Amazon Basin, but its exact area of distribution is unclear. It stands around 14 inches (35cm) at the shoulder and weighs around 22lb (10kg). This zorro is said to be mainly nocturnal and omnivorous in its diet.

Hoary zorro (*Dusicyon vetulus*)
South America
The hoary zorro inhabits the southwestern region of Brazil, where it hunts during the day in grassland and lightly wooded areas. It catches rodents and other small mammals, as well as invertebrates. The young are born in underground dens, with females often taking over the tunnels made by armadillos for this purpose.

Sechuran zorro (*Dusicyon sechurae*)
South America
Confined to a small area of the eastern part of the continent, in southern Ecuador and the adjacent region of northern Peru, this fox is named after the Sechura Desert. It is the smallest of all the *Dusicyon* species, weighing around 6½lb (3kg). It sometimes scavenges along the shoreline, but has a varied diet, being forced to survive on seed pods when other food is unavailable. It tends to be nocturnal.

Bush dog (*Speothos venaticus*)
Central and South America
Ranging from Panama down into northern South America, the bush dog looks like an otter, with a short tail and, unusually, its underparts are darker than the rest of its body. The bush dog is highly aquatic, and will hunt rodents that live mainly in water, such as the capybara (*Hydrochaeris hydrochaeris*).

Raccoon dog
(*Nyctereutes procyonoides*)
Europe and Asia
This wild dog is very similar in appearance to a raccoon. The natural environment of the species is eastern Asia, but they were released in several parts of the former Soviet Union, in the hope they would become established and could then be hunted for their fur. It has since spread in Europe, extending eastward across Germany into France. The raccoon dog tends to be nocturnal, which, combined with the fact that it does not bark, helps to conceal its whereabouts.

Eurasian Canids

These include species such as the Arctic fox which have a distribution extending literally around the world, in northern latitudes. Highly opportunistic by nature, these canids are equipped to survive in harsh environments.

1 Corsac fox
2 Tibetan fox
3 Dhole
4 Bengal fox

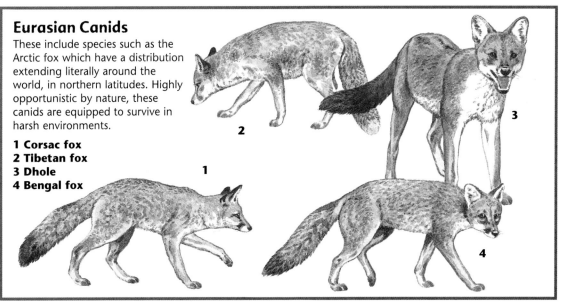

WILD WOLF TO DOMESTIC DOG
Relationships today

It is not just coincidence that most people prefer to choose a puppy rather than an older dog when they are seeking a pet. Apart from looking cute, a puppy is likely to be more adaptable and so should settle more readily into a new home. Older dogs often prove to be shyer, and there may be problems associated with them which are not obvious at first, such as aggressive behavior.

A young puppy will soon come to accept the family as its pack, and it is this ability to transfer their loyalty from other pack members to people which has led to dogs becoming such popular pets.

It is also usually possible to introduce a puppy into a home where there is already an older dog, whereas a mature dog could be a liability in such surroundings. An established dog is likely to display far less resentment toward a puppy than to a dog which is more than a year old. Having a much younger companion can help give an older dog a new lease of life. It also means that, when the time comes to part with the elderly pet, the experience may not prove so traumatic for the household in general.

Practical Pointer

When you are seeking to have a puppy as a pet, be sure to choose one that has been reared in domestic surroundings. It will be much more accustomed to human company, and to living in a home.

All these aspects of canine behavior can be related back to the social structure which exists in wolf packs in respect of the cubs. Cubs feature at the bottom of the regular hierarchical structure and are submissive in their behavior to other pack members. In turn, older wolves of both sexes treat cubs in a friendly manner.

Wolf cubs which have been reared in the company of humans lack the shyness and reserve that is associated with older individuals, in the same way that, in new surroundings, puppies are more friendly toward people than adult dogs are.

The level of aggression between the cubs in a pack does start to increase as they grow up, especially if food is in short supply, such as during the winter months. It is not necessarily a matter of dominance. At this time, fighting can be linked very closely with feeding behavior. However, when aggressive encounters are geared to obtaining sufficient food from a kill, rather than to establishing a higher position in the social rank of the pack, they quickly pass.

In domestic surroundings, when conflicts do arise, they are usually associated with food, and the dogs should therefore be fed separately to eliminate the risk of any fighting.

Practical Pointer

Always try to find out as much as possible about the background of any adult dog that you are thinking of acquiring, particularly if it is a rescued animal. It could have been rejected by its previous owners because of some serious behavioral problems, or it could have become withdrawn as a result of being neglected.

Wolf cubs show the same playful side to their natures as puppies, but they are much more wary than domesticated puppies of human contact.

Why are there domestic dogs?

The first wolves that were domesticated would have been even more unpredictable in terms of their temperament than today's hybrid dog. They would also have been much shyer. At first, there was almost certainly only a very loose association between them and the people who they lived alongside.

Some orphan wolf cubs may have been reared and remained in the vicinity of a human settlement. They probably started to join in with hunting expeditions and so a routine was established, although it would not have been possible to train them in the same way as today's dogs.

Practical Pointer

You are unlikely to find much by way of remains of ancient dogs in museums, because early archeologists unfortunately ignored their bones, concentrating instead on human finds. A lot of potentially valuable information was probably lost from many sites as a consequence, before a more enlightened attitude prevailed.

These wolves would probably have bred and remained with the family group. Eventually they would have become tamer and more trainable. The way in which they began to adapt their hunting skills, working alongside the tribespeople to achieve kills, would have ensured they were valued, even by tribal elders.

The ability of the wolves to detect danger in the dark and alert the group to any threat would also have been a great asset. There could be attacks not only by neighboring tribes, but also by other dangerous animals.

Almost certainly, the domestication of the dog did not take place at a single locality, on any single occasion. This is partly a reflection of the wide range of the grey wolf through the northern hemisphere. Doubtless, a number of wolves were kept at different stages in history, and not all would have contributed to the evolution of the domestic dog.

*This is an ancient Egyptian portrayal of the god Anubis, which has a dog-like appearance (**second from left**). Some experts suggest that this imagery was inspired by a jackal. Archeological evidence suggests that this domestication of the dog may have begun around what is now the Middle East. It was here that the origins of today's sighthounds, such as the greyhound, lie.*

Dogs for a purpose

There was a vital difference in those early stages, however, in that dogs were not kept primarily as companions. In fact, they were quite likely to be eaten if other food was in short supply. The use of the domestic dog as a source of food has continued throughout its subsequent domestication, notably in the East. The Chow Chow, for example, has been kept for this purpose in parts of China for centuries.

Dogs were also used to fulfill an enormous variety of other tasks, adapting to the changing needs of people. This has helped to ensure their continued popularity. As guns became more commonplace, in Europe for example, so a new type of dog evolved to assist in this activity. Instead of being a pack animal, like hounds, these retrievers were valued for working closely, and almost instinctively, with their owners in the field.

This Roman statue shows the wolf suckling the orphans Romulus and Remus. Legend tells how the twins founded the city of Rome, paving the way for the Roman Empire. The wolf rescued the infants from the banks of the River Tiber, and her maternal instincts led her to carry them up to the Palatine Hill and shelter them in a cave until they were found by a shepherd.

Dogs as companions

The keeping of dogs mainly as companions rather than for working purposes is a very recent phenomenon in their history that dates from the late 1800s. This developed partly as a result of the interest in the showing of dogs, pioneered by Charles Cruft, who founded the world-famous dog show that still bears his name. The interest proved infectious, to the extent that the American Kennel Club was set up in 1884 and, today, both the Westminster Show held in New York and Crufts still enjoy huge popularity.

Practical Pointer

Paintings, carvings and other artifacts portraying early domestic dogs have helped to show where particular breeds originated. There are recognizable similarities between a number of today's hounds and their ancient Egyptian forebears.

The emergence of the domestic dog

The first clear evidence of a divergence in appearance of the domestic dog has been uncovered in the Beaverhead Mountain region of the United States, in the State of Idaho. By this time, there was a small beagle-like form and a distinctly larger, retriever-sized type of dog. Their remains date back approximately 9,000 years, indicating significant variations in the size of dogs from the same locality had begun about 3,000 years after the likely start of the domestication process.

The tendency toward smaller lapdogs took place at a relatively early stage in the dog's history. Unfortunately, it is very difficult to build up any real impression of a dog's appearance, in terms of key features such as color or hair length, just from its skeleton.

While a clear indication of its facial shape can be established from its muzzle, the appearance of its ears remains unknown, because the ear flaps themselves are comprised of cartilage rather than bone. This is why the discovery of the mummified remains of dogs of terrier size in Arizona was significant. These had long coats and were black and white in color, indicating that divergence from the coloration of the grey wolf had occurred by this stage.

Hounds

In Europe, evidence from Egypt reveals that the hound lineage was established early in history. Phoenician traders were probably responsible for carrying these hounds to other localities around the Mediterranean in their ships. This legacy is still apparent today, and a number of similar hounds, such as the pharaoh hound from the island of Malta, the Ibizan hound from Spain, and the Sicilian greyhound, originating on the island of Sicily, still survive.

These three breeds all have an unmistakably similar appearance, with broad, stiff, erect ears and a short, smooth coat. In terms of their

Practical Pointer

The characters of dogs have evolved over thousands of years. If they were originally bred for outdoor work, not all will settle well in the home.
Certain sheepdogs can be included in this category.

The Ibizan hound has changed little over thousands of years. Egyptian artifacts show similar hunting dogs.

coloration, they are essentially red with white markings, which are typically confined to the vicinity of the chest. They are often considered to bear a striking resemblance to the ancient Egyptian god Anubis.

It is thought that they were first taken abroad from Egypt around 5,000 years ago and have since developed in isolation. They are athletic, agile hunters, and are able to hunt by both sight and sound, although evolution has led to other hound breeds developing other more specialized hunting skills. They have survived largely unchanged for so long because of this tendency to keep them in isolation. As a result there was little cross-breeding, which would have altered their appearance and other characteristics.

Mastiffs

It can actually be harder to trace the ancestry of other ancient breeds, although the mastiff lineage is still quite clearly defined. Dogs similar

in appearance to the Tibetan mastiff were brought westward at a relatively early period in history. In the early stages, these large, powerful dogs were aggressive by nature. They were used essentially for guarding purposes. In Europe, they were valued for their ability to protect livestock against attacks by rampaging packs of wolves, which were still numerous up until the 1800s, and beyond in some areas. Their aggressive traits were eventually turned into protective loyalties, however, and this characteristic is still markedly apparent in this breed today. They are friendly toward members of their own households, but generally prove to be aloof and very suspicious with strangers.

BASIC INSTINCTS • Wolf template

The variance in features such as coloration and size which existed in the different races of wolf through their range serves to explain the diversity which is apparent between different breeds of domestic dog. Selective breeding has reinforced characteristics of the dog's wild ancestor over the generations, creating breeds with specialist skills, such as scenthounds.

Practical Pointer

Do not be persuaded to buy a breed simply because it is fashionable. Ask yourself whether the dog would integrate well into your particular life style — otherwise you are likely to be storing up problems for the future.

Tibetan mastiff — a strong, powerful breed.

EARLY DOMESTICATION
The dog through history

Sighthounds were already present in Britain by the time of the Roman invasion, although how they reached there is a mystery. They, too, could have been brought by Phoenicians. They were apparently similar to today's greyhounds and displayed the typical lemon and white coloration associated with various breeds of hound today.

Until comparatively recently, dogs were kept primarily for working purposes, helping to hunt as in this case, or used as guardians to watch over property.

Dogs of mastiff stock were used in battle.

The Romans

The Romans valued a breed of dog called the *vertragus* highly, to the extent that a special official, known as the *procurator cynegii*, was appointed to obtain such hounds and arrange their shipment to Rome. They were similar in appearance to greyhounds and able to outrun hares, which were apparently their usual quarry.

Another type of dog already established in Britain when the Romans arrived was the mastiff, believed to have been brought by the Celts. These dogs were large, courageous and fierce, and were often used to hunt wild boar, which were an exceedingly dangerous quarry. A number were sent to fight in Roman amphitheaters, where they could reputedly kill bulls with a single blow to the animal's neck.

With the spread of Roman civilization, there was also an increasing interest in small dogs, whose main role appears to have been as companions, although they could have been used to warn owners of the presence of intruders or visitors. These were equivalent in size to today's toy breeds, measuring just 9 inches (23cm) at the shoulder.

Domestication through history: purpose-bred hounds

The reliance on hounds to assist in the hunting of game led to increasingly strict laws being placed on the ownership of such dogs, to prevent all but the aristocracy possessing them.

Middle Ages

Ironically, the hunting of the grey wolf appears to have taken on a renewed urgency at this stage, with dogs being pitted against a wolf on a regular basis throughout the Middle Ages. The natural cunning and greater stamina of the wolf meant that it was still often able to elude its domestic relative.

This period also saw the appearance of the largest breed which has ever existed. This was the Irish hound, a possible ancestor of the Irish wolfhound, which measured over 48 inches

As hunting developed, so hounds were used to catch quarry in combination with falcons. The ladies were entertained by lapdogs, so-called because of their small size. These were essentially companion dogs, although they could also serve as guardians.

(1.2m) at the shoulder. Contemporary reports describe these hounds as being a sandy shade. Hugely powerful, the Irish hound was kept both as a guardian and for hunting purposes. Its skull alone measured 17 inches (43cm) and, in terms of size, it undoubtedly would have rivalled the largest of the grey wolves.

Other dogs from this era which are now extinct include the fearsome Alaunt. These were used on the battlefield — Henry VIII of England (1509–1547) used 400 of them in his invasion of France — but, because of their ferocity, they did not survive once the invention of firearms rendered their original purpose obsolete.

Practical Pointer

Dogs will learn certain tricks, such as begging, almost instinctively, particularly if they are consistently rewarded. Poodles have a long history as circus dogs, being particularly playful by nature.

"degenerate" grouping. These apparently lacked any standardization in terms of their type, being kept instead for a variety of purposes. They included dogs which carried out tricks and danced as entertainers, and "turnspits" — small dogs trained to turn joints of meat as they roasted over open fires in the kitchens of large houses.

One breed which has survived down the centuries is the mastiff, a breed which also saw service on the battlefield. It was a mastiff that guarded the wounded knight Sir Piers Leigh on the battlefield of Agincourt in 1415.

New types of dog began to evolve too, in response to the changes taking place in society in the Middle Ages. The forerunners of today's spaniel breeds began to emerge at this stage in history, being used for hunting birds.

Classification of dog breeds

The first attempt to classify dogs into distinct varieties was undertaken in the famous work *De Canibus Britannicis*, written by an English physician, Dr. John Caius in 1570. There were hunting dogs, such as greyhounds and the so-called "limor," which was probably a forerunner of the bloodhound, that tracked its quarry by scent. Also well established at this stage were terriers and harriers, which often assisted the hunt, while spaniels and setters were fairly recent introductions.

Interestingly, it is clear there was already a movement of developing breeds from one country to another by the time that Caius's work appeared. He himself described one such black and white spaniel brought to Britain from France. Caius disliked the ladies' pets — equivalent to today's toy breeds — known then as "comforters." These small dogs were kept entirely as companions.

Some of the more interesting dogs of that period were to be found in Caius's so-called

This hunting scene clearly shows two types of hound. There are the fast, narrow-nosed sighthounds, reminiscent of a modern-day greyhound, and the broad-nosed forerunners of the scenthounds.

Practical Pointer

Today it is much easier than it was in Caius's day to prevent bitches becoming pregnant, thereby adding to the number of unwanted mongrels or cross-breds. Neutering provides the simplest solution in the long term.

Domestication through to modern times

From the late 1600s, a number of today's smaller breeds were popular at the royal courts of Europe.

King Charles Spaniel

King Charles II of England (1660–1685) actively encouraged the spaniel breed that was named after him, which actually originated in France. In those early days, these spaniels had relatively long faces, but by the 1920s, they had become much more compact.

An American spaniel enthusiast then put up substantial prize money for breeders who could produce spaniels that bore a closer resemblance to the original type. As a result, this effectively led to the emergence of two different forms of the King Charles spaniel. This recently

A King Charles spaniel — the appearance of this breed has been modified since it attracted the attention of King Charles II during the seventeenth century.

Selective breeding of hounds for their stamina took place well before the advent of dog shows. Foxhounds can be highly variable in terms of their markings.

Practical Pointer

Visiting dog shows can be a good way to meet breeders and also to learn what is involved in exhibiting. This is essentially a hobby — even a major win brings very little financial reward.

recreated form, with a longer nose more akin to the original examples of the breed, is now described as the Cavalier King Charles spaniel, to distinguish it from its flatter-faced cousin.

Foxhounds

Other breeds were changing during the 1700s, most notably the foxhound, whose history was to provide a pointer to the subsequent development of other breeds. At first, these hounds were slow and often incapable of keeping up with the fox, let alone outpacing it. Interest grew in selective breeding to improve the stamina and pace of the foxhound.

The inspiration behind this project was Hugo Meynell, who resided at Quornden Hall, in Leicestershire, England. It ultimately led to the founding of the famous Quorn pack of foxhounds.

The first dog shows also revolved around this particular breed. Masters of Foxhounds frequently took their dogs to events in the summer months, outside the hunting season. Accurate pedigree records of foxhounds extend back further than those of any other breed.

Development of the modern dog scene

More general interest in dogs in the Victorian era resulted in the establishment, in 1873, of the Kennel Club, the oldest body of its type in the world, to oversee the development of pure-bred specimens. There was also a rapid expansion of the show scene, in which selective breeding and pedigree records were to play an increasingly significant part.

The origins of the modern dog scene began in the public houses of London, the proprietors of which encouraged dog shows as a means of providing entertainment for their customers. The first major event of this type pioneered separately was a show for terrier breeds. It was organized by a pioneering dog-food salesman named Charles Cruft and took place in 1886. He had been inspired by the Paris Exhibition, and enjoyed the support of wealthy members of the aristocracy who were keen dog-lovers.

Practical Pointer

Cruft's show is now organized by the Kennel Club and attracts visitors from around the world. Each day, the different groups are judged, leading up to the finale of the Best-in-Show award on the last day.

The modern dog show scene developed at the end of the nineteenth century. Show standards exist for recognized breeds, and judges assess the dogs in accord with these prescribed features.

By 1891, Cruft was sufficiently confident to launch a more general event for breeds from around the world. He was a great showman who appreciated the value of publicity and success was virtually assured when Queen Victoria, herself a great dog enthusiast, entered some of her Pomeranians at the event.

Cruft brought together the largest selection of breeds ever assembled in one place, and the public responded enthusiastically. Not only did they come simply to see the breeds on view, but they also wanted to own them. Many of today's breeds that have since attained a strong international following, such as the Boxer, were first seen at Cruft's show.

The development of the pet-food industry on a large scale after the Second World War has since helped to simplify the care of dogs, increasing their popularity as a result. So today more and more people enter their dogs in shows or take part in dog exhibitions.

ANATOMY
Skeleton and skull shapes

The general pattern of the wolf's and dog's skeleton is very similar in terms of their components, but significant changes can be detected, most noticeably in the shape of the skull, while the length of some of the limb bones can also differ markedly. This reflects the divergence in physical appearance of domestic dogs. Not surprisingly, those which still resemble the grey wolf have a skeletal structure that most closely approximates to it.

Mutations have arisen affecting the appearance of the dog's facial shape, as well as its ears, compared with that of the grey wolf ancestor.

Skull

The dog's skull can be classified into one of three basic groupings. Those breeds with relatively long nasal chambers, such as the greyhound, which hunt primarily by sight, have skulls similar to those of the grey wolf. These are described as being "dolichocephalic."

The skull structure is altered in the case of scenthounds, or breeds such as the pointer, which have broad noses to assist in the detection of a particular scent. These are the so-called "mesocephalic" breeds.

In the case of many fighting dogs, the length of the muzzle is greatly reduced, and the upper jaw is correspondingly shorter, with the skull itself becoming more curved in shape. The lower jaw is also shortened, but not as severely as that of the upper jaw, with the result that it displays a distinct curve. This shorter, squared jaw pattern helps the dog to maintain

its grip, with more of the jaw being used for this purpose.

However, the reduction in the length of the jaws in these so-called "brachycephalic" breeds creates a potential problem, in that the teeth are likely to become overcrowded because they show no corresponding reduction in numbers. Furthermore, especially during hot weather, the severe reduction in the size of the nasal cavities leaves these breeds, as typified by the bulldog, at potentially greater risk of succumbing to the effects of heatstroke. You should try to avoid exercising any dog when the sun is very hot, but particularly these breeds.

Dogs are unable to regulate their body temperature by sweating to cool themselves — sweat glands are restricted to the area between the toes, where they serve more as scent-

Practical Pointer

Dogs are more likely to make a mess when eating if they are forced to use their teeth to rip their food apart, so when feeding fresh or canned food, break it into reasonably small chunks.

Some breeds such as the Alaskan malamute retain a strong affinity with the wolf, in terms of their facial appearance and underlying skull structure. Other breeds from the far north like the Siberian husky share similar features.

markers. Instead, to dissipate heat, dogs rely on a combination of panting and the cooling effect of water evaporating from their nasal cavities. The latter is essentially no longer possible in the case of the brachycephalic breeds.

The pattern of dentition in wolves and domestic dogs, indeed in the whole family, is surprisingly constant. They generally have 42 teeth, which, with the exception of the molars, are paired. The incisor teeth at the front of the mouth are curved, and help the dog to maintain its grip, while the pointed canines at the corners of the mouth can be used to overpower prey. They are blunter than in some other carnivores, such as cats.

There is then a gap, called the diastema, leading back to the chewing teeth, which comprise the premolars and molars. The molars are unpaired, with two at each side of the upper jaw and three beneath, at each side of the lower jaw, so that the last premolar above can work in association with the first molar in the lower jaws, to shear through meat. These are sometimes called the carnassial teeth.

Dogs will use these teeth to chew their food, as demonstrated when they hold their head down to one side. Dogs prefer to gulp their food, like wolves, rather than chewing it into small pieces. This is a reflection of pack life, where eating as much as possible in the shortest period of time can make the difference between survival and death.

In the case of other breeds, the skull shape may be broadened and slightly shortened, compared with that of the wolf. The enlargement of the nasal passages helps to improve the dog's scenting skills, and so it is most apparent in dogs such as the pointer.

Certain breeds show a more dramatic shortening of the skull, as exemplified by this bulldog. The nasal passages are greatly compressed, to the point that such breeds are susceptible to heatstroke, as dogs cool themselves by loss of moisture from the nasal cavities.

Tail docking will alter the appearance of a dog permanently, with part of the tail being removed. This surgery is carried out soon after birth. The Pembrokeshire Welsh corgi puppy on the left has been docked, with its litter-mate retaining a full-length tail.

The breastbone, or sternum, is located at the front of the chest and extends along the lower side of the body, where it provides support to the rib cage. It is not a rigid structure, however, because otherwise the chest wall would lack the flexibility to move in and out as the dog breathed. Nor are all the ribs attached to the sternum. The last pairs, the so-called "floating ribs" are free of the sternum and are slightly shorter.

Behind the thoracic vertebrae, and running along the back above the abdomen, are the dorsal vertebrae, which may vary from six to eight in number. They are characterized by broad, raised vertical projections on their upper surfaces, known as the dorsal spines. These provide for the attachment of muscles, to assist the dog's movement. They also restrict the mobility of the spinal column, concentrating the dog's power into running or jumping.

Further stability follows behind, where the sacral part of the vertebral column attaches to the hips, enabling the thrust from the powerful hind limbs to be maximized into movement.

Vertebral column

One of the main reasons why dogs cannot climb effectively is because of the structure of their spinal column. It lacks the mobility of that of cats, and so restricts the dog's movements, although both wolves, and indeed dogs, can run at pace for relatively long distances if necessary. Yet, while the wolf may be seen as the general blueprint, there has been a trend toward specialization in the case of domestic dogs, which in a few instances has been potentially counterproductive.

The skull attaches to the vertebral column by means of the seven cervical vertebrae. These in turn are linked to the 13 thoracic vertebrae that form the upper part of the chest wall. The ribs extend from here down the sides of the body. The actual shape of the chest varies somewhat, according to the breed of dog. In those which are most active and have a high oxygen requirement, such as the borzoi, the chest is deep, to provide room for a large lung capacity and a suitably powerful heart to pump the blood around the body.

Practical Pointer

When dealing with a dog which has suffered intervertebral disk problems, be sure to restrict its mobility. Otherwise the outlook for recovery will be bleak. Never encourage dachshunds (a breed predisposed to this condition) to jump, or to climb up flights of stairs.

Intervertebral disks

Sandwiched between the vertebrae themselves are intervertebral disks, which act rather like shock-absorbers. Degeneration of these disks at an early stage is especially common in dachshunds, which have relatively long backs. Should the disk rupture, it will impinge on the spinal cord, causing a variety of symptoms, which may include paralysis, depending on where the rupture occurs. The most likely sites are at the thoracolumbar junction and in the cervical region.

Tail

It is at the rear end of the vertebral column that the greatest variation is to be seen, in the case of the bone structure of the tail. There may be between 14 and 23 coccygeal vertebrae, which narrow along their length to the tip of the tail. In the case of the domestic dog, some breeds have a naturally short tail, which is described as a bobtail, but in other cases, the tail length is deliberately shortened by a process called docking. This entails cutting off a variable length of the tail when the dog is very young.

Proponents of docking argue that, in the case of working breeds, this saves the tail from being injured later in life. Those who are opposed to the concept highlight the fact that docking may be painful, even for a puppy, and that dogs use their tails as a means of communication.

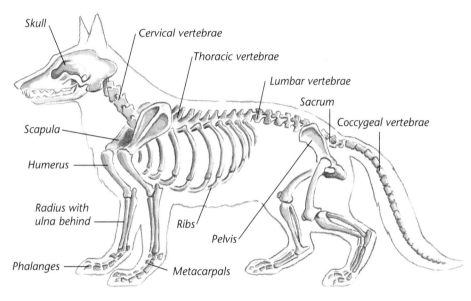

The skeleton of the majority of dogs is basically the same, although there may be slight variations, most notably affecting the shape of the skull. It does not differ greatly from that of the grey wolf. The ears are not built around bone, but are comprised of cartilage.

Sighthounds such as the greyhound have a particularly athletic build, as the sprinters rather than the distance runners of the dog world.

Limbs

The wolf depends largely on its superior speed to overtake and kill its quarry. Injured wolves are unlikely to survive for long in the wild, particularly if they cannot keep up with the rest of the pack. They will then face a slow death from starvation. It is therefore not surprising that the domestic dog has inherited its ancestor's ability to run, and shows the same skeletal adaptions for this purpose.

Forelimbs

Dogs lack a functional collar bone because this would allow energy to be wasted by pulling the limbs laterally. Binding them tightly against the body increases the power of the propulsive thrust. The collar bone, or clavicle, is still present, however, but reduced to a thin wafer buried in the muscle mass in the shoulder region.

One of the features of the wolf, and of most other dogs, is that their legs are long in relation to their bodies. This allows them to cover more ground per stride. The flattened shoulder bone, or scapula, contributes to the length of the limb, and also the dog's stride, because it is bound tightly against the body.

Stride length means that some dogs cover much more ground with a single bound than others, when running at speed. A deep chest provides good lung capacity.

The scapula attaches to the humerus beneath, while lower down the limb are the radius and ulna. Increases in the length of these bones can also be seen, while greater stability results from the tight binding together of radius and ulna. These form the wrist at their lower end, with the metacarpal bones (which are also found in our hands) actually forming part of the dog's limb, rather than its front paw, and increasing its length as a result.

The dog supports all of its weight on its digits and, as a result, is said to run in a digitigrade fashion. The pads on the underside of the digits are tough and horny, absorbing any unevenness and roughness of the ground as the dog runs over it, although profuse bleeding is likely to follow if a pad is cut, typically on a piece of glass.

There are obviously other bones present in the lower part of the limbs, and these are also

Practical Pointer

Cases of hip dysplasia often lead to osteoarthritis in later life. This may need treatment with painkillers, although today, in severe cases, it is possible to carry out hip replacement surgery successfully.

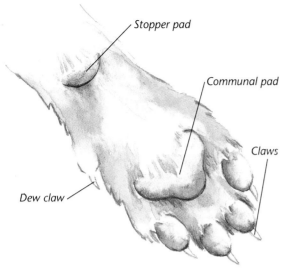

Stopper pad

Communal pad

Claws

Dew claw

A dog's paw seen from beneath. The stopper pad gives support and prevents the dog from losing its grip on a slippery surface. The pads may appear tough, but are highly vascular and will bleed profusely if cut.

bound together tightly with ligaments to prevent any sideways movement. The only exception to this type of pattern in the whole canid family is found in the tree-climbing fox, in which rigid forelimbs would make climbing impossible. Greater rotation of the bones means that these foxes are capable of grasping and adjusting their position off the ground, so they will be less likely to fall and injure themselves.

Hindlimbs

In the case of the hindlimbs, the upper bone, known as the femur, fits into the hips, forming a ball-and-socket joint. In domestic dogs, typically those weighing over 24 pounds (11 kg), there may be a developmental weakness which causes the socket to be too shallow. This results in the condition known as hip dysplasia.

The bottom of the femur, where it forms the knee joint, is more likely to be a point of weakness in the smaller breeds. This particular joint is quite flexible, being required to allow the dog to jump effectively, with the major thrust coming from the hindlimb. If the knee-cap slips, however, this creates the condition known as luxating patella.

The tibia and fibula in the hindlimb extend down to the ankle joint, with the structure of the lower part of the dog's hindlimb being not dissimilar from that of its forelimb. Stability is equally important here.

Some breeds, such as this basset hound, have short legs. This group of hounds arose in France and are used by huntsmen on foot. "Basset" is derived from "bas" meaning "low" and refers to the short legs.

Shortening of the limbs as in the basset hound (above) has occurred without any corresponding reduction of the body. The length of their legs means that jumping is difficult, and should not be encouraged. This also applies in the case of the dachshund (below). Their vertebral column is quite weak, and they can be prone to intervertebral disk problems as a result.

Practical Pointer

Dew claws, when present, need to be trimmed back regularly. Since they are not worn down by contact with the ground, these claws have sharp points and continue growing, to the extent that they may even curl around and grow into the pad, which can be very painful for the dog.

Changes resulting from domestication

The incidence of skeletal problems is much higher in domestic dogs than in wolves. In the wild, natural selection pressures would ultimately prevent wolves that were suffering from congenital disorders, such as hip dysplasia, from making any significant input into the gene pool. A disability of this type would result in their acquiring lower social status, and so they would be unlikely to mate within the hierarchy of the pack.

There are no such constraints with domestic dogs, and as breeding of closely related stock is not uncommon, in order to preserve and even improve on desirable features, there is a risk of emphasizing the effects of harmful genes — as can be seen in breeds such as the dachshund.

Leg length

One of the most significant changes in appearance within the domestic dog group, compared with wolves, is the emergence of dogs with dramatically shortened legs. These are frequently described as bassets, this name being derived from the French word *bas*, meaning "low." The size of the rest of the body in these dogs shows no alteration.

The various dachshunds are also short-legged, with long bodies, for functional purposes. This enables them to disappear underground without difficulty, where they were formerly used to pursue badgers, whereas this would be virtually impossible for a hunting dog with longer legs.

Claws and toes

There are also differences in claw structure between wolves and domestic dogs. As with the reduction in the length of the legs, what might well be harmful to the wild wolf has advantages for the owners of domestic dogs, and so such traits have been encouraged.

In all cases, however, the dog's claws are not retractable, being broad and generally blunt-ended. They serve to anchor the feet into the ground as the dog runs, helping to prevent it from sliding over. But although dogs have five toes, the innermost of these, equivalent to the human thumb, is held permanently off the ground. It can be used by the dog to hold down quarry if necessary, and is called the dew claw simply because it skims the grass, picking up the moisture of dew.

An increase in the number of toes — known as polydactylism — is a notable feature of the Lundehund, or Norwegian puffin dog, which may have six toes on each foot, as well as extra dew claws. This assists these dogs as they climb around the sheer cliffs of their Norwegian homeland, hunting for nesting puffins.

Wild dogs lack dew claws on their hind legs, but these are a common feature in domestic breeds. The briard actually has double

Practical Pointer
Short-legged dogs are not adept swimmers, so keep them away from deep stretches of water, where they might encounter difficulties if they fell or jumped in.

dew claws, which are considered to be characteristic of the breed. Because of this, they cannot be removed, but in other breeds, these claws are often excised early in life. Otherwise the dog may become caught up and tear the claw as a result.

The lundehund or Norwegian puffin dog is unusual because it often has more toes than other breeds and extra dew claws, which help to give a better grip.

COAT VARIATIONS
Development of colors and textures

All the colors seen in domestic dogs are present to a variable extent in the coats of wolves. Selective breeding of dogs has seen the emergence of breeds characterized by their so-called "self," or pure, colors. The range of colors available extends from white through shades of red to brown and black. So-called "blue" colors are the result of a combination of black and white hairs running through the coat.

Self coloring may be broken by small areas of white on the bodies of the darker-colored dogs, typically on the chest, or there may be more widely distributed white patches, a feature associated particularly with hounds. Wolves, too, can often be identified from a distance by their markings, but self coloration in wolves is very unusual. The Newfoundland white wolf (*Canis lupus beothucus*), which was white in color, as its name suggests (although in reality was a subspecies of the grey wolf), was the notable exception. It was finally hunted into extinction in 1911.

The natural coloration of the wolf is influenced to a large extent by the terrain in which it lives, and helps to provide camouflage. The tundra race of the grey wolf (*C. l. albus*), for example, has a much paler coat than the typical grey wolf (*C. l. lupus*), which used to range widely through the forests of Europe. There, dark coloring would help the wolves to blend in against the shadows of the trees. In desert areas, wolves with sandier-colored coats are likely to be encountered. Therefore, in spite of its name, the grey wolf occurs in a wide range of color variants.

In the case of the dog, as domestication has proceeded, so the coat in many cases has become longer. This would be a handicap to a wild wolf, as its fur would soon become matted

The coloration of many hounds is distinctive, being either tricolored as shown in the dog above, or bicolored. The markings are sufficiently distinctive to enable individuals within a pack to be identified without difficulty.

BELTON (*English setter*)

BLACK AND TAN
(*Hamiltonstövare*)

BLUE
(*Basset bleu de Gascogne*)

BRINDLE (*Greyhound*)

GRIZZLE
(*Old English sheepdog*)

HARLEQUIN (*Great Dane*)

PARTI-COLOR
(*Swedish vallhund*)

PIEBALD (*Dalmatian*)

RED (*Irish setter*)

ROAN (*Welsh corgi*)

TRICOLOR (*Beagle*)

WHEATEN
(*Soft-coat wheaten terrier*)

This is the lemon and white form of the beagle.

and dirty. It is important to remember that long-haired breeds, such as the Afghan hound, need considerable grooming every day in order to maintain their immaculate appearance.

Other hounds, such as the beagle and foxhound, have short coats. This is partly because they regularly hunt in overgrown terrain where the long hair of the Afghan would be a distinct handicap. The coloration of these short-coated hounds of northern European origin is frequently tricolored — being black, white and tan — or sometimes lemon and white.

BASIC INSTINCTS • Wolf's thick coat

The coat also serves to protect the wolf from climatic extremes. The coat consists of two layers. There is the longer top coat, made up of coarse guard hairs, and a shorter, dense, insulating layer of hair beneath. The coat is of even length over the body, including the tail, with the weather-resistant guard hairs standing away from the body. The coloration of the grey wolf is variable, as shown below in these two individuals.

Unusual coats

There are some dogs which have a highly distinctive appearance, simply because they have virtually no coat.

"Hairless" dogs

A mutation has occurred giving rise to so-called "hairless" breeds, which do actually have some body hair, most noticeably on their heads. The origins of these breeds are something of a mystery, but they probably arose quite early during the domestication process.

The Chinese crested dog is the best-known example, but there are also Mexican and Peruvian hairless dogs. The skin coloration of hairless individuals still gives a clear indication of their coloration, with pink patches indicating what would otherwise be areas of white hair.

Litters typically consist of both hairless and normal-coated puppies, the latter being

Above *Hair is confined to the extremities of the body in the case of the hairless form of the Chinese crested dog. The pattern of pigmentation seen in the skin depends on the individual.*

described as "powder-puffs". Hairless dogs are a good choice for owners who tend to be allergic to animal fur in general, although obviously the care of such dogs is slightly different to that of other breeds.

In the first place, they are susceptible to the cold as a result of their lack of hair. The lack of hair can have a less obvious effect, however, particularly when the weather is hot. These hairless breeds are at risk of suffering from sunburn, because their skin is so exposed, especially in the case of those with pale bodies. Sunblocks will be needed and these dogs should be kept indoors as much as possible when the sun is at its hottest.

Above *This is the powderpuff form of the Chinese crested dog — one of a number of the so-called hairless breeds.*

Practical Pointer

Hairless dogs that have pink skin are more vulnerable to sunburn than those with dark skin, because, in these pale areas, there is no protective melanin pigment present.

Wire-haired dogs

Another coat variant which has become established in the case of the domestic dog is the wire-haired form. This is associated with a variety of breeds, ranging from dachshunds and various terriers to larger dogs, such as the wire-haired pointed griffon. The coat of these dogs is coarse and wiry, as the name suggests, and provides them with good protection In undergrowth, being relatively impenetrable to thorns and other sharp projections.

The wire coat does not lie sleek against the skin, nor will it be molted as usual. This means that the dead hair here will have to be stripped out at least twice a year. Further trimming is often required prior to a show. While more frequent stripping of pet dogs of this type will be needed if the coat is basically clipped, rather than being dealt with by hand in the traditional but time-consuming manner.

Molting

Not all dogs actually molt their coats — poodles being a typical example. This may be helpful in terms of keeping the house clean, but instead the coat will need to be clipped about every six weeks or so. This may prove to be

Practical Pointer

It is not just hairless breeds that may need protection against the elements. A number of thin-coated hounds, such as the whippet and Italian greyhound, should be fitted with a jacket to protect them from extreme weather. Dog jackets are sold on the basis of length, so measure your pet's back to obtain the correct size, or better still, take your dog along for a fitting!

an extra expense, unless you feel confident enough to carry out this task for yourself.

Other breeds shed hair often throughout the year, although the peak molting times are in the spring, when the dense winter coat, most apparent in northern breeds, is lost, to be replaced by a lighter summer coat. Another period of molting then occurs in the autumn, as the winter coat starts to grow.

Wire-haired variants have been developed in some breeds such as the dachshunds. This change in coat texture gives better protection in undergrowth.

EVOLUTION
Breeds and selective breeding

Changes in the appearance of domestic dogs have occurred because of various mutations which, in the first instance, affected coat length, face shape, and similar features. Geneticists believe that just 20, or even fewer, such primary changes could account for the wide diversity apparent in the various breeds of dog which now exist.

Selective breeding has also subsequently played a part. It is likely that there have been as many as 5,000 generations of domestic dog since the domestication process began, enabling desirable features to be developed and emphasized. Dogs started to evolve distinctive types long before the onset of dog shows, but these events have proved to be the major factor responsible for the standardization and division of dogs into today's breeds.

One of the forms of the Belgian shepherd dog, known as the Tervuren, named after the region of Belgium where it was developed.

Defining a breed

What defines a breed is now laid down in the breed standard. This specifies the ideal "type", or appearance, of that particular breed, to the extent that, in the show ring, dogs are not judged against each other, but with respect to the standard. The dog which is considered to be closest to the ideal will win the class.

Not all breeds are recognized for show purposes, however, usually because they are either very scarce in a particular country or are a new breed that has yet to achieve standardization in appearance. Also, the number of new breeds being created today is relatively small. One of the most recent is the kyi leo, which, in spite of its name, is of North American origin, having been developed in California. It was evolved from crossings of Maltese and lhasa apso stock as a companion breed suited to an apartment life style.

Today, throughout the world, there are between 350 and 400 different types of domestic dog. However, as some are added to this list, so equally, others are becoming extinct, like the Tahltan bear dog, bred by the Tahltan indian tribe of North America.

Popularity of breeds

It is something of a mystery as to why some breeds manage to attain a strong international

Practical Pointer

Try not to be too influenced by the latest trends when selecting a breed. It can be harder to obtain good-quality stock of a fashionable breed, simply because unscrupulous breeders may be tempted to produce as many puppies as possible to meet the increased demand, without worrying about the dogs' welfare.

Variations in coat length have been emphasized in the domestic dog, as shown by the smooth collie (above) and the long-haired collie (below), but they are also apparent in grey wolf populations as well.

following, whereas others remain highly localized. The shepherd dogs of Europe are an example. All are believed to share a common ancestry, but while the German shepherd dog (formerly known as the Alsatian) is one of the best known of all breeds, the Belgian shepherd dog group is far less common. Meanwhile the Dutch shepherd dog is virtually unknown outside its homeland.

Fashion does undeniably, and possibly increasingly, play a part in the relative popularity of the different breeds. The "Lassie" character, for example, generated a huge following for the rough collie breed, while more recently the film *"101 Dalmatians"* has led to considerable interest in this breed.

PROTECTING RARE BREEDS

There is a growing awareness on the part of dog-lovers today to conserve the rarer breeds. One of the great success stories in recent years has involved a Chinese breed called the Shar Pei. The plight of this ancient breed was brought to the attention of American breeders by the writings of Matgo Law, in the dog press. Stock was taken to the United States in the late 1970s and reached the United Kingdom in 1981. Since then, the breed has become well established outside its southern Chinese homeland, and its future is now secure.

Possible weaknesses

Domestic dogs show far more diversity in both appearance and size compared with cats. This is in part a reflection of the fact that the grey wolf naturally shows a much greater variation in size through its range, and this trait is apparent in domestic dogs today, with such divergence being encouraged by selective breeding.

In the case of the poodle, for example, the standard variety was scaled down, resulting first in the miniature poodle and subsequently the toy poodle. Loss of soundness does appear to be a problem, however, once the dog's size falls dramatically. Many small breeds are at risk from luxating patellas (kneecap) in the hindlimbs (see page 31).

Selective breeding has, of course, meant that a number of today's breeds would have difficulty in reverting to a free-living existence.

Scaling down in size has led to breed weaknesses becoming more apparent in breeds like the miniature poodle. Generally however, small dogs have a longer life expectancy than their larger relatives.

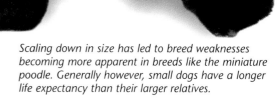

The Siberian husky retains a similarity to the grey wolf, partly because it has not been subjected to the same selective pressures as breeds from elsewhere in the world.

Interestingly, the domestic dogs that most closely resemble the grey wolf are those which are still kept essentially for working purposes in northern areas, such as the Siberian husky.

Sled dogs have another feature in common with their grey-wolf ancestor — they are kept in groups and so their behavioral patterns have not altered dramatically. In many ways, they live much as the early wolf-dogs would have done. Even their coloration in many cases clearly resembles that of the wolf.

Nevertheless, members of this group can suffer from various genetic and congenital disorders. Siberian huskies, for example, are known to suffer from Von Willebrand's disease, which is a disorder affecting the blood-clotting system, so that blood loss following injury, or even as the result of a season in a bitch, can be both unduly severe and prolonged.

A large number of these type of problems have been recorded, with at least one disorder of this type, and frequently more, being associated with the majority of breeds. Thankfully, the incidence is generally low, but the effects can be serious in some cases. While breeders may be aware of the vulnerability of their particular breed to specific complaints, it may prove a difficult task to trace the incidence of the affected genes within a bloodline. By the time a puppy is born with a hereditary defect, it could well be that the genes responsible have been widely distributed, making other cases more likely to arise in future generations.

Screening programs involving breeding stock are being set up wherever possible to lessen the likelihood of these genes being passed on from one generation to the next. Already the results with hip dysplasia and progressive retinal atrophy, a disorder affecting the cells of the retina at the back of the eyes, have led to a noticeable decline in these widespread conditions.

While it is often said that mongrels are healthier than pure-bred dogs, this is not necessarily true. Any canid — wild or domestic — is likely to be equally vulnerable to the major infective illnesses, such as distemper, if not protected by vaccination. The incidence of inherited afflictions is, however, far lower in the case of mongrels.

Practical Pointer
You can tell the likely adult size of a mongrel puppy by looking at its feet. Large paws at this stage indicate that the puppy will grow up into a relatively large dog.

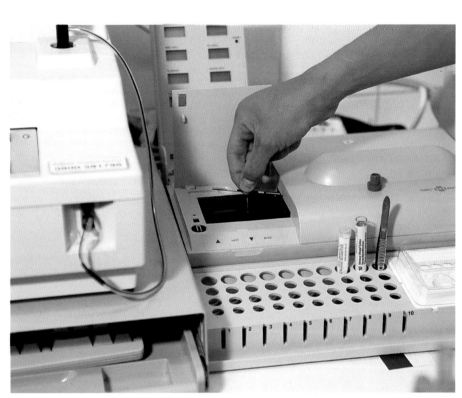

There are now various ways of screening dogs for potential breed weaknesses, depending on the likely type of problem concerned. Skeletal weaknesses may be highlighted by X-ray examinations, whereas metabolic problems can be checked by laboratory tests of different types.

Practical Pointer
If you are seeking a relatively quiet breed, the basenji would be a good choice. It is sometimes called the barkless dog, although, in reality, it is not silent but sometimes utters strange yodeling and chortling calls.

HYBRIDS
From folk tales to science

Few animals are capable of inspiring so much terror in people as the grey wolf. Fear of wolves has been etched into human consciousness over the course of generations and reinforced by childhood stories, such as *"Little Red Riding Hood"*. But now, at last, with the wolf largely eliminated from much of its former range, there are signs that this situation is changing, especially in North America.

It is the unpredictability of grey wolves which can make them dangerous, and particularly if they are cornered, then they are likely to attack. Wild wolves infected by rabies are especially dangerous.

The truth is that attacks by wolves on people have always been decidedly uncommon, even when the numbers of wolves were far higher than today. Partly struck by guilt over the way that wolves were trapped and killed, often needlessly, people have begun to reappraise their relationship with the wolf.

Wolves have already been reintroduced into areas where they were previously eliminated, and "wolf-watching" has become a popular pastime, especially in parts of North America. Unfortunately, however, this new-found affinity with the wolf has also had less desirable consequences.

Practical Pointer
Do not be tempted to consider a wolf-dog hybrid puppy, no matter how cute it may appear. Such hybrids will be a dangerous liability and you could well find yourself in court if your wolf-dog injures or even kills someone.

Hybrids
The genetic links between grey wolves and domestic dogs remain today, to the extent that they can breed together successfully and produce hybrid offspring. This has already occurred in some parts of the wolves' former range in Europe, where just a handful of them still survive. They have mated with domestic dogs, usually strays out scavenging on garbage dumps and similar sites, to which the wolves are also attracted by the prospect of food.

Some breeders have sought to produce deliberate hybrids by pairing captive wolves with established breeds, typically those of northern stock, such as the Alaskan malamute, which resemble the wolf most closely in appearance, but have far more stable temperaments. Such wolf-dog crosses have become quite popular in the United States,

This grey wolf is four months old, and looks similar to a puppy. Dogs are easy to train but wolves remain intractable even if attempts are made to train them from an early age. They are more nervous especially if kept on their own rather than with other wolves.

BASIC INSTINCTS • Coydogs

Male coyotes do mate quite readily with domestic dogs, however, producing what are often described as "coydog" offspring. In many cases, these hybrids actually appear to be more tractable than those bred from wolves, although they may be unpredictable in terms of temperament and can still be aggressive. Some coydogs do respond to training though, and often have a friendly side to their natures, particularly toward those who they know well. It may seem strange, therefore, that grey wolves and coyotes do not themselves hybridize where they occur together in the wild. There appears to be a strong antipathy between them, certainly on the part of the wolves, which will often kill their smaller relatives. Nevertheless, successful hybridization between these two species has been carried out on at least one occasion, in zoo surroundings.

especially over the past decade, to the extent that an estimated 500,000 or more are now being kept there.

However, whereas the wolf itself has a natural caution with regard to people, these hybrids tend to lack such reserve and may readily attack as a consequence, particularly once they are mature. Even greater problems with aggression in such hybrids is likely if domestic dogs bred primarily for guarding purposes, such as rottweilers, are used. Many American states have banned wolf-dog hybrids, which have already been responsible for the deaths of a number of people.

Hybrids may result from the matings of domestic dogs with other species of the genus *Canis*, which are their closest relations, but, as a rule, these are uncommon. They take place in areas where there are a large number of stray dogs. Cross-breeding with foxes, however, does not appear to be a viable option because they are not so closely related.

This is a Saarlooswolfhond — a breed that was created by the reintroduction of wolf genes to a domestic dog lineage during the 1930s.

Practical Pointer

Hip dysplasia is one of a number of inherited problems for which breeding stock is now commonly screened. The larger breeds, such as the German shepherd dog and labrador retriever, are especially vulnerable — only buy from reputable breeders whose stock has been screened. Otherwise, before long, your young dog is likely to be displaying signs of hindlimb weakness, depending on the degree to which the hip joints are affected.

Saarloos's program

Wolf-dogs are not a new phenomenon, and the legacy of such hybridization can be seen in Europe today. During the 1930s, a Dutchman named Leendert Saarloos, working together with a local zoo, began a special breeding program that was to entail the cross-breeding of grey wolves and domestic dogs.

Saarloos believed that the domestic dog had become weakened by selective breeding over the course of many generations, and that this had led to problems such as hip dysplasia. His aim was to eliminate these faults and introduce vigor into the domestic dog by hybridizing it back to its original ancestor.

He chose the German shepherd dog for this purpose, but his theory received a serious setback in its early stages when the original wolf

Practical Pointer

Always be sure to establish a clear impression of a breed's likely temperament and needs before making any decisions. Dogs do differ significantly in such respects, with sled dogs, such as Siberian huskies, being strong and athletic, and requiring plenty of exercise.

he selected for the program died of a viral infection, that it had possibly contracted from its canine companion.

Later he encountered behavioral problems in the wolf-dog puppies that resulted from the second pairing. They were less responsive to training than domestic dogs and were also shyer by nature. They also proved keen to roam and displayed a strong pack instinct.

Saarloos continued with his breeding program, concentrating on reducing the lupine (wolf) influence over successive generations by pairing the offspring repeatedly back to German shepherd dogs. The intention was that wolves would play no further part in the breeding strategy after the first pairing.

The undesirable traits which Saarloos originally observed had largely disappeared by the time of his death in 1969. Other enthusiasts subsequently took up the challenge of his work. Six years later the breed was finally accepted for registration purposes by the Dutch Kennel Club. It was given the name of its creator and so became known as the Saarlooswolfhond. Saarloos's own belief, which originally led to the development of the breed, remains unproven.

Today, these dogs can be seen at major European dog shows, but they are not common. They are carefully protected by their supporters from any possible threat of exploitation as a result of their ancestry, and are far removed from today's wolf-dog hybrids in terms of their temperament.

Nevertheless, they do still retain a slightly withdrawn side to their natures, especially toward strangers, and are often most settled when kept in pairs rather than as single companions, reflecting the influence of the wolf's recent genetic input into their development.

The German shepherd dog was the other contributor to the development of this breed. Saarloos believed its vigor was declining and sought to remedy the situation by hybridization.

DOMESTICATION
Where breeds originated

The origins of today's dog breeds owe much to the former distribution of the grey wolf. The majority are from the northern hemisphere. Relatively few have come from Africa, where the grey wolf never ranged. The notable exception is the basenji, a hunting dog from Central Africa, which is probably descended from the early Egyptian hounds. More recently, in the late 1800s, the Rhodesian ridgeback was bred in the south of the continent by Boer settlers. The distinctive raised ridge of hair running down its back is a feature inherited from the extinct Hottentot dog.

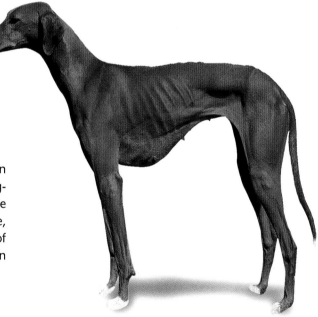

Other probable descendants of the Egyptian hounds are the azawakh, a very fast, long-legged breed, kept by the Tuareg tribespeople in the southern Saharan region to hunt gazelle, and the sloughi, also from the northern part of Africa and now becoming better known in other parts of the world as well.

South America
A similar situation exists in South America, which is the other area that is uninhabited by wolves. There are the ancient Peruvian hairless dogs, which may be related to the Mexican hairless breed occurring further north. Recognized breeds from further south, such as the Fila Brasiliero and Dogo Argentino, are of much more recent origin, with an ancestry relating to breeds brought there from other parts of the world.

North America
Companion breeds are virtually unknown from North America, where it was essential that dogs

The lean, fit appearance of the azawakh means that its ribs show — like the greyhound, this North African breed carries no body fat. It has good lung capacity.

Practical Pointer
Breeds which originated in other parts of the world are generally no more difficult to manage than those that evolved in the region where you live, but you may have to provide them with extra protection in the winter if the weather is cold.

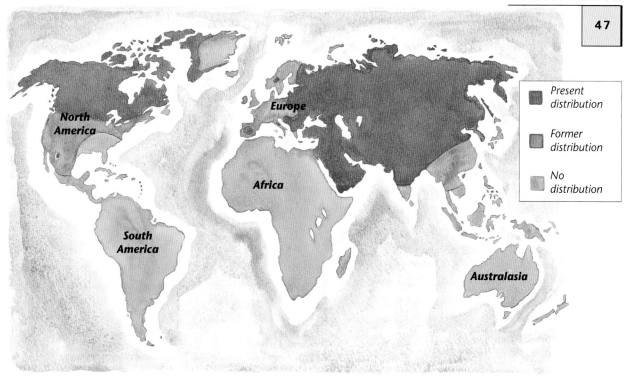

This map shows both the former and current ranges of the grey wolf, revealing how its distribution has been curtailed in recent times, particularly in Europe. The distribution of the wolf helps in turn to explain the pattern of evolution of the domestic dog.

Present distribution

Former distribution

No distribution

were able to work alongside people, hauling sleds or tracking game in what was, and still can be, a particularly harsh environment, where only the fittest survive.

The power of these dogs, working in teams of six, is quite phenomenal. Alaskan malamutes regularly pull sleds weighing over 700 pounds (355kg) for distances of over 50 miles (80km) a day.

Eurasia

It was in Europe and Asia, where life was more settled, that the toy breeds were developed. These breeds were strictly protected in many cases, with ownership being confined to the nobility. At the Imperial Palace in Beijing, the

The Dogo Argentino — a South American breed developed from imported European stock in the 1920s. Relatively few breeds of dogs have originated on this continent.

Pekingese was guarded to the extent that anyone who was caught trying to smuggle one of these dogs out of China faced certain death. It was only after British forces stormed the palace that this breed was seen in the West for the first time.

Few dogs can ever have led such a pampered existence as the Pekingese. They were sometimes called "sleeve dogs", as they were small enough to be carried in the flowing sleeves of courtiers. Their puppies were even wet-nursed on occasions.

Today's Pekingese have more compact faces and longer coats than their Chinese ancestors.

Practical Pointer

New breeds are usually obtained by breeders in the first instance, because of the need to import at least several dogs so that unrelated bloodlines can be established. Subsequently, surplus stock may be sold as pets, but new arrivals are usually costly to purchase, because of their relative rarity compared with established breeds.

The lineage of the domestic dog is thought to stem from several distinct lineages of wolf, which occurred through North America, Europe, the Middle East and Asia.

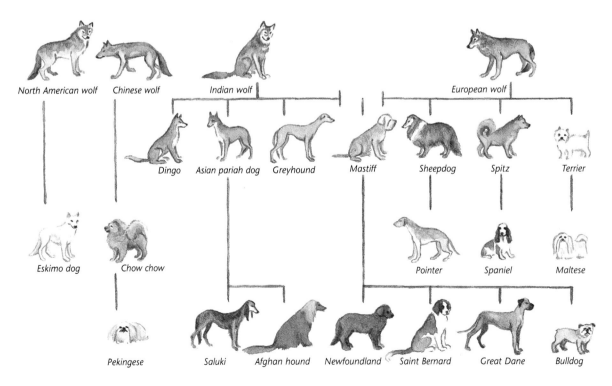

BASIC INSTINCTS • Sled team
Dogs served as a vital means of keeping communities in touch, never more so than in the case of Nome, in Alaska, when it faced a diptheria outbreak in the early 1900s. With no other means of reaching this outpost, it took the bravery of a sled team to get through under the most appalling conditions.

BREED GROUPINGS
How are breeds defined?

The classification of breeds for show purposes differs somewhat from one country to another. Under Kennel Club rules for example, there are five basic divisions, comprising gundog, hound, terrier, toy, and utility groupings. The situation in North America is somewhat different, with non-sporting and sporting sections, and no separate utility or gundog categories.

There are also considerable differences in the recognition of breeds, and, in some cases, even in the breed standards themselves. The greatest number of breeds is recognized by the European body called the Féderation Cynologique Internationale (FCI), which has also sought to divide breeds more on the basis of their functions. In most cases, the dogs in each category have features in common — in terms of both their appearance and temperament.

The Chihuahua is accepted as the smallest breed in the world, and is kept as a companion. It is classed as a toy breed. This is the long-haired variant.

The hound group

The hound group traces its ancestry back to the earliest days of the domestication of the dog, in the vicinity of the Middle East. While the older breeds tend to hunt by a combination of sight and sound, just like wolves, there is also evidence of increased specialization within the group. The sighthounds, as epitomized by the Afghan hound and the greyhound, are highly athletic, with a long, loping stride. A so-called "roach back" is typically seen in this type of hound, which slopes noticeably from the shoulders down to the hips.

Since their sense of smell is of relatively little significance, the nasal chamber of these sighthounds is narrow, giving their head a rather pear-shaped appearance. Although built for speed, these hounds also have stamina and are sure-footed, being able to turn at speed to prevent their quarry from eluding them.

Sighthounds are independent rather than pack dogs. As pets they are active and lively

The Irish wolfhound is the largest breed of dog in the world. With its hunting ancestry, its breed is classified as a hound.

Classification of dogs only began with the development of the show scene toward the end of the nineteenth century. There were various types of bulldog in existence at that stage.

companions. Early training can be difficult because they are prone to follow their instincts, and run off readily. Ex-racing greyhounds are often offered as pets once their career on the track is over. They will prove to be gentle dogs, and are very trustworthy with children.

It is a good idea to muzzle such hounds when taking them for a walk, however, particularly where they might encounter other smaller dogs, which they may instinctively regard as potential quarry. Greyhounds tend to be sprinters and, after a brief burst of running, they will be content to return home. This makes them a good choice if you do not have a lot of time each day to walk a dog.

Scenthounds are built for stamina rather than speed. Their noses are broad, to maximize their abilities to follow a trail. Often working in packs, such dogs are friendly and boisterous, as well as gluttonous, and are often very ready to steal food.

Today's bulldog is rather different in appearance, with a larger head and shorter legs than its ancestors.

Practical Pointer

Lurchers are not a standard breed of hound, but the result of cross-breeding between greyhounds and collies, frequently for poaching purposes. This is why many Lurchers are traditionally dark-coated, to conceal their presence at night.

Terriers and toys

Both these groups are comprised of small breeds, but they can show a remarkable difference in temperament. Terriers tend to be tough, wiry, tenacious characters whereas many toy breeds are much more docile and compliant, having been bred essentially as companions. While the vast majority of terrier breeds originated in Britain, the origins of toys are much more diverse.

Terriers

In many cases, terriers were originally bred as hunt companions. They were required to drive foxes and other creatures out of their burrows, so that the hounds could then pursue their quarry. Faced with a determined and cornered fox within the confines of a burrow meant that such dogs needed to have a bold and brave nature. It is no coincidence that many terriers have wiry coats, because originally they spent much of their time outdoors.

Another feature of terriers is their ability to kill rodents, to the extent that, in the

Rats were a health hazard and hunting them was a vital activity that terriers could be relied upon to undertake with enthusiasm. Even pet terriers will still instinctively catch and kill these rodents today.

Other dogs such as the Staffordshire bull terrier were pitched against each other in vicious dog fights that often resulted in death for one or both dogs.

nineteenth century, rat-killing contests used to be held in London public houses. A leading ratter of the period, named Billy, managed to kill a hundred rats in just six minutes and thirteen seconds. With increasing urbanization at this stage in history, terriers became much in demand as a means of curbing the growing rodent populations.

The bravery of terriers was also used in a far more negative way, in the form of dogfighting contests. Staffordshire and English bull terriers were kept for this purpose after bull-baiting itself was banned. Even today, these particular terriers will not agree well with others of their kind, and can be a liability in areas where there are many other dogs.

More recently, the notorious pit bull terriers, which have been responsible for many vicious attacks on people, have shown the undesirably aggressive side of these dogs. Restrictions on their ownership have been introduced in a number of countries, although the situation has been made difficult because these terriers are not a recognized breed. Rather, they are cross-breds, being a combination of a bull terrier and often a rottweiler, or similarly dominant breed.

Toys

Members of the toy group include the tiny Chihuahua, named after the Mexican province of this name where the breed is believed to have originated. Its origins are now obscured, but it occurs in both a long- and short-coated form. A distinct anatomical peculiarity that is associated with the Chihuahua is its open molera. The roof of the skull is not fully formed, to the extent that an opening can be cautiously discerned under the skin. In behavioral terms, this breed is also unusual in that it will shiver when nervous or excited and not just when it is cold.

A number of scaled-down versions of larger breeds are also to be found in the toy category. This includes the very popular Pomeranian, which is one of the smallest members of the spitz group,

The Pomeranian is the smallest member of the Spitz group of dogs, complete with a fox-like face.

whose members bear the closest similarity to the grey wolf.

The Pomeranian itself stands around 11 inches (28cm) high, only slightly smaller than the shamanu, or Japanese wolf (*Canis lupus hodophilax*), which was hunted to extinction around 1905. It measured 14 inches (39cm) tall, and was mainly a pale shade of grey.

Many of the Oriental breeds which still survive today are in fact in the toy category, although there is no evidence to suggest that they are descended from the shamanu wolf. It is only quite recently, however, that such breeds have become well known in the West. Both the Tibetan terrier (which, in spite of its name, is not a terrier) and the Lhasa apso, also from Tibet, were first seen in the West in the 1930s. The pugs, Pekingese and shih tzu are also of Oriental origin.

Toy breeds usually have appealing personalities and develop into loyal companions. They often prove to be alert and courageous guardians as well. In spite of the problems of soundness, these small dogs generally have a longer life expectancy than their larger relatives.

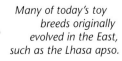

Many of today's toy breeds originally evolved in the East, such as the Lhasa apso.

Herding dogs

The use of dogs to protect livestock against predators is an ancient tradition that extends back to the early days of farming. Herding dogs can be divided into two categories. The larger breeds, such as the Bergamasco from Italy, or the Tibetan mastiff itself, are primarily flock guardians. These often worked in the company of smaller dogs that were actually responsible for controlling the animals.

The true herding breeds were evolved mainly to work with sheep and goats. Across Europe, a number of such breeds evolved in isolation and, in some cases, are quite dissimilar in appearance. One feature that they do tend to have in common, however, is the water-resistant nature of their coats, as they would be outside working in all weathers.

Old English sheepdog

The Old English sheepdog is one of the best-known members of this group internationally, with a long, shaggy coat that needs daily grooming to prevent it from becoming matted.

In common with other sheepdogs, the Bergamasco is a lively and intelligent breed that will not thrive if kept confined in urban surroundings. Behavioral problems will inevitably develop under these circumstances.

Dogs have been used for herding and guarding stock for centuries, and working sheepdogs in particular are a common sight in many countries.

Welsh corgis

Some herding dogs have been evolved to work with cattle rather than sheep, and perhaps surprisingly, these are often smaller in size. The Welsh corgi is a typical example, measuring just 12 inches (30cm) in height. There are two different types — the Cardigan, which has a long tail resembling that of a fox, and the Pembroke, also named after a county in Wales.

They are both old breeds, dating back centuries, and bear a strong resemblance to the Swedish vallhund, although the relationship between these breeds is unclear. Their small size is advantageous, because it means they can move easily among the cattle, encouraging them to move forward by nipping at their heels, with relatively little risk of being kicked, which could obviously have fatal consequences.

Corgis once played an important part in driving herds of cattle to market, but unfortunately their tendency to nip is still apparent in the breed today, and they may respond almost instinctively in this way on occasions. Firm training from an early age will deter this type of behavior, but even so there are probably other breeds better suited to a home with children.

Australian herding dogs

Herding dogs with excellent stamina and adaptable natures were required to work in

Australia and one of the best-known breeds evolved for this purpose is the Australian cattle dog. It is slightly larger than the corgi, measuring up to 20 inches (51cm) high at the shoulders. A wide selection of breeds is thought to have contributed to its ancestry, including possibly the dingo, as well as the Dalmatian, which is why Australian cattle dog puppies are white at birth.

While the dingo helped to contribute the required stamina, its semblance to a wolf-dog hybrid means these dogs are not responsive to training. The Dalmatian, bred to trot beside the carriages of the rich in Britain and elsewhere, has a more malleable nature, as well as the ability to cover large expanses of ground at a fair pace.

Another Australian herding breed with an interesting ancestry is the kelpie. These sheepdogs are descended from a pair of collies, sent out from England in 1870, that produced puppies on their arrival. In due course, one of these then mated with a local dog, which was called kelpie.

Various colors, ranging from shades of red to brown, are seen in the case of the Australian kelpie. Black dogs in this instance are called barbs, although they are in fact the same breed. Like all good sheepdogs, they have the ability to control the sheep not so much by running around after them as by using their eyes and fixing them with their gaze.

One member of this group becoming increasingly popular on the international show scene at present, is the Australian shepherd. Confusingly, however, this breed has actually been developed mainly in the United States, with its origins lying in France and Spain.

The Australian cattle dog is a tough, hardy herding breed, with excellent stamina.

BASIC INSTINCTS • Adapted to heat
The fennec fox is a type of wild dog that is found in hot, arid climates. There is no cover for hunting purposes, so it relies on its large ears to locate rodents and other creatures that it can catch. The fox has to hunt after dark when the temperature is much cooler. During the heat of the day, it often hides away in burrows or rocky outcrops.

Working dogs

This is one of the most diverse categories, corresponding roughly to the utility breeds featured in the Kennel Club classification. As a result, the members of this group have a range of backgrounds and have been used for a variety of purposes. It is therefore particularly important to look into the breed history very carefully, in order to gain a reliable indication of the dog's likely temperament. A number of these breeds are now no longer kept for their original purpose and are at risk of dying out, unless they attract the attention of dog-lovers.

Spitz breeds

Already the Tahltan bear dog has disappeared from North America,

The Karelian bear dog is a hunting companion, bred in Finland. In contrast, the doberman (below) is a breed developed primarily as a guardian, and still retains a rather dominant nature. Both may be considered to be working breeds.

The Swedish elkhound is very similar in appearance and coloration to a grey wolf. It is the largest of the elkhound breeds that are native to Scandinavia.

while in Europe, a similar breed, the karelian bear dog, underwent a decline in numbers in the 1960s. It is named after the province of Finland where it evolved. Today, this striking black and white breed has undergone a revival in numbers and its future is much more secure.

Similar spitz-type breeds from Scandinavia, characterized by their pricked ears, resembling those of wolves, and a well-furred tail that will curl to one side of the body when the dog is standing. They have been kept in this part of the world for centuries, as multi-purpose dogs used to herd stock as well as hunt. Some, such as the Swedish elkhound, which stands up to 25 inches (64cm) tall and is the largest member of the group, have a coloration similar to that of the grey wolf.

An alert disposition combined with a friendly nature is a feature of these dogs, which means that, in more recent times, they have appealed to those seeking a companion breed. They are not always as well disposed toward others of their own kind.

Rottweiler

A number of the working dogs are large and powerful in build, as typified by the Rottweiler. This breed is very popular in many countries, especially the United States, having originated in the German town of Rottweil during the last century. Standing up to 27 inches (69cm) at the shoulder and weighing 110 pounds (50kg), it is a formidable guardian when aroused, and firm training is essential from puppyhood to keep its aggressive tendencies under control.

Doberman

The Doberman, another German breed, is often similarly colored to the rottweiler, with black and tan markings, and a sleek, short coat. It has a narrower muzzle, however, and a lighter build. Bred originally to protect a tax collector called Louis Doberman, this breed is potentially aggressive toward those whom it regards as strangers, although great efforts have been made by breeders to remove this particular trait from its character.

Dobermans which show any indication of this behavior in the show ring will never be among the winners. But it is vital that this type of dog is kept under control at all times, and never left alone in the company of children.

St. Bernard

Other working breeds are recognized for their friendly dispositions, in spite of their large size. Among them is the St. Bernard, which can weigh as much as 200 pounds (91kg). Its origins can be traced back over 1,000 years, to the Hospice of St. Bernard de Menthon, in the Swiss Alps. The nearby treacherous mountain pass claimed the lives of many travelers and these large dogs were used to rescue those in difficulties. Over the centuries, they are reputed to have saved more than 2,500 lives.

The St. Bernard first attracted attention because of its mountain rescue skills, and it is now a popular pet worldwide, in spite of its tendency to dribble.

Gundogs (sporting dogs)

A range of today's most popular breeds of dog are to be found in this grouping. This is not entirely surprising, because they were evolved to work at close quarters with people, and so are very responsive to training, as well as being friendly by nature. Although shooting with guns did not become widespread until the 1800s, the ancestry of a number of these breeds goes back much farther. Prior to this, dogs such as spaniels were used to locate and then retrieve birds, such as waterfowl for example, that had been shot with bows.

Water dogs

One of the characteristics of many members of the gundog grouping is their readiness to enter water. While wolves themselves are able to swim, they tend not to do so unless for a particular reason. It may seem hard to believe, based on its appearance, but the poodle was originally bred as a retriever. The manicured and distinctive coat associated with the breed stems from this era.

The limbs, especially the area around the joints, were shaved of fur to assist the swimming abilities of these dogs, but much of the hair on the body was left, to give better

A curly-coated retriever. Its dense coat again helps to trap air close to the body, so the dog does not become rapidly chilled in cold water.

insulation against the cold water. Leaving the hair long on the tip of the tail meant that it was easier to watch the poodle's progress.

Wildfowling abilities are apparent in a number of these sporting breeds, including the curly-coated retriever. Like the poodle, it also has a dense and tightly curled coat. The curls are most apparent on the body, with the legs again being used to assist the dog to swim well. The tapering tail acts rather like a rudder.

The third representative of this group with a curled coat is the Irish water spaniel. The advantage of this type of coat structure is that it is relatively water-resistant. As a consequence, the dog can shake much of the water out of its coat when emerging onto land and thus can continue working without risk of being chilled.

Pointers

The keen scenting abilities of the pointer have been valued for centuries. Its role is at the start of the search for game. Part of its amazing scenting skill is thought to have come from crossings involving bloodhounds.

Apart from the pointer itself, there are a number of similar breeds that originate from various European countries, such as the large French pointer, the German wire-haired pointer, and the old Danish pointer. Many of

An Irish water spaniel – it has a dense water-repellent coat, not unlike that of the poodle which may be descended from this ancient breed.

The pointer has a broad nose which means that it has an acute sense of smell and, once it has located potential quarry for the hunter, it will then pause and adopt its characteristic position, effectively pointing out the direction of the creature.

"setter" is derived from an old English word "set", which means "sit" and describes the way that these dogs respond having scented game. Setters have broad heads and relatively long coats, with longer hair, known as "feathering", present on the back of the front legs and along the underside of the tail.

Spaniels

Smaller in stature are the spaniels, which, today, are often kept purely as pets, although they are equally at home as working gundogs. There has been a divergence in type, with show dogs having more profuse coats than their working counterparts. They are used to flush game and also to retrieve.

Golden and labrador retrievers

The most adaptable gundogs are the golden and labrador retrievers, which are now among the most popular breeds in the world. Their scenting skills and intelligence are applied in many different situations, both in the home and elsewhere. They may work as guide dogs or hearing dogs and are equally suited for working in airports seeking out drugs or explosives. In the field, they are still used as retrievers, while their responsive, lively personalities also make them popular as family pets.

these still remain localized in distribution, even within their country of origin. This applies particularly in France, where a number of different Pointer breeds are to be found.

Setters

Another group that has evolved because of its ability to locate and indicate the presence of game is the setter, many of which, particularly the Irish setter (often incorrectly called the red setter), are now popular as household pets. The name

PURPOSE-BUILT SWIMMER

In the case of some gundogs, the feet have become modified to assist their swimming abilities. The Chesapeake Bay retriever, named after the area of the United States where it was developed in the 1800s, has webbed toes for this purpose, combined with very powerful hindquarters. Its coat is relatively smooth but oily, which again protects against waterlogging and chilling.

Feral dogs

Around the world, there are a number of feral dogs. These are domestic dogs which have reverted back to an independent, free-living life style, as distinct from strays seen on city streets.

Dingoes

The dingo is the best-known example of a feral dog, and is believed to have been taken to Australia by the early Aboriginal settlers. It is now clear, however, that the links between dingoes and the Aborigines are not as strong as previously thought. These dogs are generally tolerated rather than encouraged by the Aboriginal people, and do not play a significant role in their culture. This may be because dingoes have proved almost impossible to train.

Their ancestry remains a mystery, but there are a number of similar dogs to be found further north in Asia. As might be expected, dingoes show considerable variation in size, as they are not a standardized breed and they have now diverged from their ancestral roots.

One of the features of the dingo which is distinctive is its coloration — this is a reddish-brown shade, often with white markings on the underparts. Subtle changes are occurring,

The dingo has been hunted heavily in Australia because it is blamed for attacking sheep. These feral dogs are thought to have been resident in Australia for more than 8,000 years.

however, because of hybridization between dingoes and other dogs in parts of their range.

There are several significant anatomical differences which set dingoes apart from domestic dogs. The most obvious is probably the fact that their canine and carnassial teeth are larger, while in temperament dingoes are relatively quiet, notably when hunting. This may be because, in many areas, they do not associate together like wolves. Instead, they rely on an element of surprise to achieve a kill, rather than on the collective abilities of a pack.

However, where there are packs, the structure is similar to that normally associated with wolves. There is a matriarchal hierarchy, to the extent that only the dominant female will breed. If another female in the pack becomes pregnant, the matriarch will kill her rival's pups. Unlike most domestic breeds, dingoes come into season only once a year rather than twice. Mating usually occurs in March or April, with as many as ten young being born nine weeks later. It will be around six months before they are fully independent.

The New Guinea singing dog is kept in a state of semi-liberty around settlements on that island. Some of these dogs are now being kept and bred in the U.S.

Dingoes have been heavily hunted because of the damage they might inflict on Australia's sheep industry, especially at lambing time, but, in reality, they prey readily on the country's native animals, such as wallabies.

New Guinea singing dog

On islands to the north of Australia, similar feral dog populations are found, and these are attracting interest from dog-fanciers. Currently, the best known of these is the New Guinea singing dog, although others can be found on New Ireland and elsewhere. It, too, has a reddish coat, often broken with white markings, and an unusual, almost melodic call.

Canaan dog

Feral dogs are sometimes also known as pariahs. In the Middle East, successful repeated domestication has occurred, resulting in the emergence of the Canaan dog. The breeding program began in 1935 in Israel, and Canaan dogs are now kept in many countries. Their appearance has become standardized, but they retain the features of a typical pariah dog.

Their ancestors were probably first kept around 4,000 years ago, to guard herds of goats from predators, such as jackals. As a result, they are quite amenable to training and this has helped to ensure their popularity.

BASIC INSTINCTS • A tough life

Many dogs live in a state of semi-liberty in places such as Africa. They often have to forage for much of their own food, but benefit from being in contact with people as well, since they receive shelter and some care. This particular dog, drinking at an African water hole is in poor condition. Many such dogs are heavily infected by internal and external parasites, and they are vulnerable to illnesses which they may acquire from their wild relatives. Not surprisingly, their life expectancy tends to be lower than that of truly domestic dogs.

The Canaan dog is a breed which, having lived in a feral state, has now been domesticated again.

EARLY

LIFE

The social coherence and pack structure of the grey wolf is one reason why the domestication of these wild canids proved to be successful. The domestic dog has effectively transferred its allegiance from the pack to people, although there is a key socialization period early in a puppy's life that is vital to its future development. If deprived of contact with people at this crucial stage, it will prove difficult to win the dog's confidence as it grows older. The hierarchy that exists within a pack means that a young puppy will normally adapt well to domestic surroundings, and will be eager to win approval from its owner and other members of the family.

BREEDING
"Heat" in seasons

Domestic dogs in general tend to reproduce more prolifically than the grey wolf. Bitches usually have two periods of reproductive activity, known as "heats," each year, whereas female wolves only come into season once. However, there are breed differences, with the Basenji, for example, generally having only one heat annually. This often occurs in the fall, rather than in spring or summer as in most breeds.

The basenji displays the typical reproductive pattern of the grey wolf, with bitches coming into season just once a year, rather than twice like most domestic dogs.

There are differences between individuals, and also a variance due to latitude. The basenji, unlike most breeds, originates from equatorial areas, where there are no significant seasonal distinctions. In contrast, breeds from the far north, and wolves living in this area, benefit from coming into heat in late winter. The pups are then born in late spring or early summer, when the climate is likely to be favorable for their survival and prey easier to acquire.

The importance of factors such as climate is now far less important to domestic dogs, simply because, in most cases, they are no longer dependent on obtaining their own food, nor on the temperature.

Bitches will come into heat throughout their lives, beginning at around six months. Smaller breeds mature more rapidly than larger ones, probably because they attain adult size at an earlier stage. Large dogs may not have their first period of heat until they are over a year old.

It is not recommended to allow a bitch to mate until her second heat at the earliest, which means, in the case of a larger breed, she could be approaching two years old before she has her first litter of puppies. Although she will have two periods of heat each year, the bitch should not be allowed to have more than one litter in a year, because of the demands of raising the puppies.

Male dogs mature at a similar age to females, although there are significant breed differences — with male beagles, for example, usually attaining maturity at a much earlier

Practical Pointer

Check that male dogs, especially toy breeds, have two testicles in their scrotum. It can happen that one is retained within the body, giving rise to the condition known as cryptorchidism. This requires surgical correction, since the retained testicle can give rise to a Sertoli cell tumor.

stage than females. Even so, it is inadvisable to use them for breeding purposes until they are at least a year old.

Domestic dogs are usually more promiscuous than wolves. If unsupervised, they will mate at the earliest opportunity, which is why a bitch on heat must be closely chaperoned to prevent her from becoming pregnant. Only in a very few breeds, notably those developed largely in isolation, such as the saluki from North Africa, is the bitch likely to reject the advances of dogs other than her own breed.

BASIC INSTINCTS • Mating wolves
In the case of wolves, it is likely to be only the dominant pair which actually mate. Young animals which have just attained puberty, and therefore are at a relatively low level in the social hierarchy of the pack, are unlikely to be reproductively active.

By concentrating all the pack's resources on one litter of cubs, there is an increased likelihood that a significant number of them will survive to maturity. If there were many cubs, the pack would be likely to face difficulties in finding sufficient food and chaperoning a group of cubs of different ages.

Male and female cycles

Although male dogs can mate at any time of the year, they will only attempt to do so when the female is on heat. Chemical messengers, known as pheromones, are produced by the bitch at this time and serve to attract males. These molecules are wafted in the breeze and can carry a considerable distance, which is why male dogs may be drawn from afar when there is a bitch on heat in the neighborhood.

Onset of heat

The earliest visual indication of heat is swelling of the vulva, and a blood-stained discharge which originates from the uterus. In contrast to menstruation, this bleeding precedes ovulation. The blood loss is variable, but can usually be detected on the bitch's bedding. She will also spend longer than normal licking her hind-quarters at this stage.

Although a number of male dogs may be drawn to a bitch in heat, it will be the dominant individual, not necessarily the biggest dog, who will mate with her.

Practical Pointer

Be particularly careful with a bitch in season, because her desire to mate may be so strong that she will slip out of the garden in search of a mate. Do not allow her out unsupervised.

Her behavior also alters, and she becomes more playful, encouraging the male's interest. However, male dogs which do approach at this stage will not be permitted to mate while the bitch is still in pro-estrus. This typically lasts about nine days and, subsequently, the bitch then enters the estrus phase, during which copulation is likely to occur.

Estrus and ovulation

As estrus proceeds, so the vaginal discharge changes from being bloody to becoming clearer. Instead of bounding away when approached by a male, the bitch will stand with her tail to one side of her body, indicating a readiness to mate. She will not necessarily

accept all dogs which approach her. She has to perceive the male as being more dominant than herself, as occurs in the case of wolves.

Ovulation itself usually takes place within a few days of the beginning of estrus, but because there is no accompanying increase in temperature, as there is in humans, it cannot be detected easily. As a result, breeders tend to mate bitches twice between the tenth and fourteenth day from the start of the breeding cycle, in order to increase the likelihood of a successful mating.

Mating

The male clasps the female tightly during mating. In most cases, a so-called "tie" is formed, in which the swollen tip of the male's penis is anchored into place by the muscles of the bitch's vagina. The bone in the dog's penis helps to provide rigidity during the mating process.

The spermatozoa are ejaculated at an early stage, after which the male, still inside his partner, switches position. He drops down off her back and swings round so that, ultimately, their hindquarters are together while their heads are pointing in opposite directions.

As with the wolf, this serves to provide more safety at what is a vulnerable time for both dogs. During this period, which can occasionally last for over an hour, secretions from the prostate gland are released into the

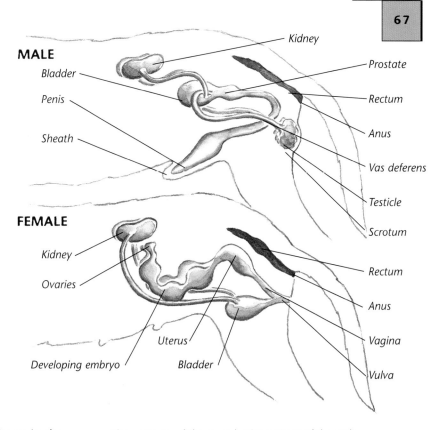

The anatomy of the reproductive systems of the male dog (top) and the bitch (bottom). The female in this case is already pregnant, with signs of the developing fetuses already evident as swellings in her uterus. Whereas the bitch's genital opening is at the rear of her body, it is located underneath the body in front of the hindlimbs in the case of the male.

female's reproductive tract, which enhance the prospect of fertilization. Finally the dogs separate and clean themselves.

It is not strictly essential for a tie to take place in order for fertilization to occur, and in certain breeds, notably the chow chow, a tie is unlikely to be formed. In any event, avoid separating the dogs during mating, because this could cause injury. Once they are tied, it is too late to prevent any transfer of sperm and you will need to arrange for the bitch to have a special injection if you wish to prevent her conceiving puppies.

Practical Pointer

Bitches may mate repeatedly during estrus, so do not allow your bitch to wander, even after mating, because she may well seek another mate. The puppies in a litter may be the offspring of more than one father.

Pregnancy

Assuming that mating is successful, pregnancy is likely to last approximately nine weeks. In other cases, the signs of estrus will subside, usually after a period of roughly two weeks, so that the period of heat extends for just over three weeks on average. There will then follow a lengthy anestrus phase, lasting perhaps five months or more, until the next period of heat.

Signs of pregnancy

It is difficult to tell for the first month whether or not mating has been successful. During this stage, the fertilized eggs move down the oviducts to the uterus, which has a short body and long horns. This is because there are normally a relatively large number of puppies and the horns actually provide a means of accommodating them all successfully.

The fertilized eggs implant into the wall of the uterus, where they develop a placental connection. The placenta serves to nourish the puppies as they grow. In the early stages, do

This sheepdog is near the end of her pregnancy, with her nipples being more prominent than usual. She gave birth to 12 puppies. Wolves may have up to 11 offspring although 6 is probably an average litter.

not be tempted to prod the bitch's abdomen to see if you can feel the pups because this could cause a fatal injury.

Obvious signs, such as abdominal distention and swelling of the mammary glands, become apparent about five weeks into the pregnancy. This parallels the situation in the wolf, where the physical growth in size of the cubs occurs in the final stages, so as to minimize the encumbrance to the female, who still needs to keep up with the pack and hunt.

Care of the bitch

During most of the pregnancy, the bitch will not require any special treatment. She can be allowed to exercise normally, which will help to maintain her muscle tone, but toward the end of the gestation period, she should be discouraged from jumping. Only in the latter stages, when the puppies are growing in size, is she likely to require additional food.

It is better to offer her extra food in the form of additional meals, rather than simply increasing the amount of food given in her regular feeding schedule, because her abdomen will already be distended by the presence of the puppies. You should seek advice from your veterinarian about the amount of food she will require. It is also important to deworm the bitch to lower the risk to the puppies of early infection.

It is important to choose a quiet area in the home where the dog can give birth and the puppies can be reared through to independence. The kitchen can be too busy

Practical Pointer

It is quite normal for milk to appear at the nipples prior to the puppies being born. Equally, pregnancy may vary in length, extending for up to seventy days without necessitating any cause for concern, although a veterinary check-up under these circumstances is recommended.

Wolves are very vulnerable as cubs, and the mother may need to move her offspring from potential danger, carrying them individually in her mouth.

and may be positively dangerous, especially when cooking is taking place, unless the puppies are duly constrained. The bathroom may be an alternative, but here again, there will inevitably be disturbances at certain times of the day. A spare bedroom is the ideal situation, if available, although you must be prepared to cover the floor with a sheet of linoleum or similar material that can be easily cleaned.

WHELPING BOX

A whelping box is recommended for when the bitch is ready to give birth and this should be made available to her during the last ten days of pregnancy. The box should be large enough to allow her to lie out comfortably. It should have a barrier extending about 3 inches (7.5cm) around the sides so that there will be no risk of the bitch crushing her puppies soon after birth. This can be a particular problem with some of the larger breeds. Easy access to the box is important, so the sides should be correspondingly low, while ensuring that the puppies will be securely contained. Line the box with a thick layer of newspaper, and before the puppies are due, put in an old blanket, or similar bedding, to encourage the bitch to sleep there.

Birth

Female wolves and domestic dogs both seek a quiet haven when the birth is imminent. Wolves may use a cave or a similar den, while a dog, if she dislikes the position of the whelping box, will seek another locality. There is little point in trying to dissuade her under these circumstances, although you may be able to compromise by moving the whelping box to the part of the home which your bitch prefers.

Restlessness is one of the most likely signs that birth is really imminent, and a bitch also sometimes loses her appetite and vomits at this stage. Other indicators include swelling of the vulva, which also becomes a darker shade of pink. Immediately prior to the birth, you may also notice that the pelvic ligaments slacken, so that the upper points of the hips appear more pronounced.

Birth process

In the vast majority of cases, birth proceeds without problems, although the bitch may appear to be rather distressed, particularly if she has not given birth before, frequently panting or even shivering. When the puppies are soon to be born, abdominal contractions become

It is vital that puppies start suckling without delay after being born, because the first milk or colostrum contains protective antibodies. These border collie puppies are just a day old.

In the case of the grey wolf the average size of a litter comprises six cubs although there may be some variation. The gestation period for both wolves and dogs is similar, usually lasting 63 days.

a similar size at birth. The upper limit for a litter for smaller breeds of dog is six pups, while up to fourteen puppies may be born to large bitches.

Problems

Should you suspect any problems during the birth process, contact your veterinarian for advice. One of the most common is a breech birth, when the puppy is born tail first rather than head first. It can become stuck in this position, with fatal consequences unless it is freed without delay. Some breeds, notably those with large heads, such as the bulldog, are more prone to difficulties in giving birth than others.

quite apparent. The puppies themselves are produced head first, often with the allantoic sacs surrounding them still intact.

The bitch instinctively breaks this sac with her teeth and then licks the puppy to start it breathing. Should the puppy still be attached to its placenta, via the umbilical cord, she will also bite through and sever this connection. Once the birth process begins, the puppies are born in quite rapid succession, typically at about thirty-minute intervals.

Placentas

It is important to count the placentas, which will be expelled after each puppy. These are usually eaten by the bitch — such behavior is quite normal and not indicative of impending cannibalism. Female wolves behave in the same way because, by disposing of the afterbirth, there is less to attract predators to the den. Should the placentas be retained in the body, this can give rise to a serious infection.

Litter size

Where there is a difference, however, is in the numbers of offspring produced. Larger dogs, with bigger reproductive tracts, have larger litters than smaller breeds, but all puppies are of

BASIC INSTINCTS • Security

Both wolves and domstic dogs seek out a quiet spot where they can give birth. Caves or underground retreats are favored by all wild dogs for this purpose. Here the offspring can remain in relative safety while their mother seeks food, or water, which is vital in order to maintain a sufficient flow of milk. The young will remain in close proximity to each other at first, to conserve their body heat.

GROWING UP
Young puppies

Healthy puppies grow surprisingly fast. Their eyes will begin to open when they are about a fortnight old and their hearing will be effective in a further week. Their mother will watch over them closely at first, attending to all their needs while they are helpless. By licking them, she regulates their body functions until they are about three weeks old and starting to move around on their own.

Puppies will be keen to explore, and this is the stage during which they are most likely to encounter problems. It is possible that this young dog could end up with a flower pot stuck on its head for example.

This is also the stage at which the puppies are likely to start eating on their own, although it will still be several weeks before they are independent. At this stage, in common with her wild relatives, the bitch is likely to respond by vomiting food for them. This is quite normal behavior, and not a cause for concern. Vomiting food may also be easier for the puppies to digest, as it will have been exposed to digestive juices in the bitch's stomach (although the majority of enzymatic action occurs lower down the digestive tract, in the small intestine).

Weaning
The attitude of the bitch to her puppies will change from this stage onward. She will spend less time with them and will discourage them from suckling, so they will be more inclined to switch to solid food. Her milk output also declines as the puppies suckle less, but it will not be until they are about six weeks old that their first teeth start to emerge.

Puppies are all weaned at a similar age, in spite of the difference in the size of the various breeds. The main divergence in growth rate

actually takes place in the post-weaning period. The diet for puppies from this stage onward is therefore important; they will need on average about twice the amount of food compared with an adult dog of the equivalent weight.

Choosing a puppy
When it comes to choosing a puppy, it is quite usual for the litter to be viewed before they are independent. Purchasing direct from the breeder provides much greater insight into the background of a puppy. One which has been reared in domestic surroundings is likely to be instinctively more friendly than a young dog that has lived in kennels throughout its early life. There is actually a crucial period, often described as the socialization phase, lasting from the first three to fourteen days of the puppy's life. If the young dog does not have any close contact with people at this stage, it is likely to remain shy throughout its life.

When choosing a puppy, there are several aspects to consider, such as whether or not you want to exhibit your pet in the future. A puppy from show stock is likely to be correspondingly more expensive than one bought from an ordinary pure-bred dog, which may be slightly mismarked for example, which would make it unsuitable for the show ring.

If you are concerned about breeding from your puppy in the future, then obtain a bitch. You can arrange for her to be mated with a suitable stud dog in due course. Bitches may prove more affectionate than dogs and are also less likely to stray, but you will have the problem of their periods of heat to cope with, unless they are neutered.

A healthy puppy

Healthy puppies tend to be very lively when they are awake, but they will also sleep for long periods. This is quite normal. Their skin is loose and pliable, and they should feel plump. Their eyes should be clear, with no sign of any discharge onto the surrounding fur at the time of weaning, and their ears should be clean.

Check the coat for any signs of parasites (see page 121) and also check under the tail — any staining here is indicative of diarrhea. This need not necessarily be a cause for concern as it can be linked with a deworming treatment. The puppy should move about freely and also needs to be alert.

Right *When picking up a puppy, the most important thing is to restrain the hindquarters properly, to prevent the young dog from struggling. Puppies should be lifted up regularly from an early age, so they become used to the experience and then will not resent it in later life.*

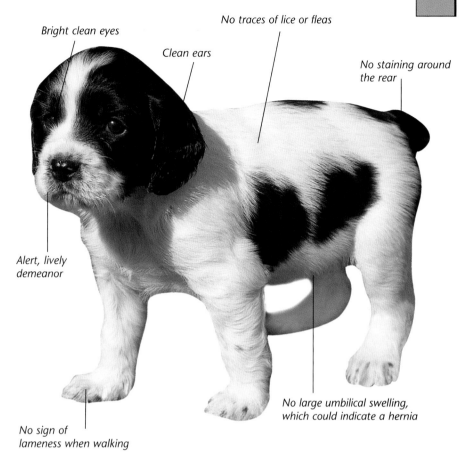

Bright clean eyes

Clean ears

No traces of lice or fleas

No staining around the rear

Alert, lively demeanor

No sign of lameness when walking

No large umbilical swelling, which could indicate a hernia

Above *An English springer spaniel at five weeks old.*

SETTLING IN AT HOME
Puppy principles

Having arranged to collect your puppy, ensure that all the preparations are made at home in advance. Obtain a diet sheet from the breeder, setting out the feeding regimen to which the puppy has been accustomed, and obtain similar food for it, at least at first. This will greatly lessen the likelihood of any serious digestive upset. You can then introduce changes gradually as your puppy settles into its new home with you.

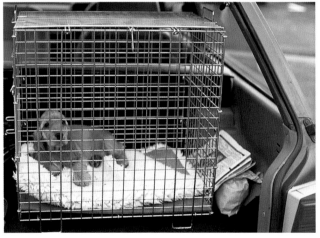

Being able to travel with your pet safely and securely restrained in the car is vital. This type of carrying cage can double for transport purposes, simply needing to be lined with old newspaper and a blanket on top.

Transporting your puppy
Rather than allowing a young puppy to sit on your lap on the way home, a special traveling crate is recommended. This will also be useful when taking your new pet to the veterinarian, for example, and, in the case of a small breed, it should suffice throughout its life. Larger breeds should be housed behind a dog-guard in the back of a station wagon. It is never a good idea to allow a dog freedom in a car, because of the risk of it distracting the driver and causing an accident. Also, a young dog left on its own in a car might be destructive and could rip up the upholstery.

At home
When you first arrive home with your new puppy, be prepared to allow it to sleep, as it will probably be tired. You can then start to accustom it to its new life with you. Puppies are naturally more adaptable than older dogs. In the wild, young wolves will themselves split off from the family group and wander on their own for a time before joining with another pack.

If you already have an older dog, then introducing it to a new puppy needs to be carried out carefully, to avoid conflict. Your

Practical Pointer
It can help to have your dog microchipped as a second means of identification. The microchip unit, about the size of a small grain of rice, can be inserted under the dog's skin by your veterinarian. It contains a unique code, which can be recognized by a special reader passed over this area of the body. This helps should its medallion be lost.

Puppies often play boisterously, but if you also have an older dog, supervise them carefully, to prevent a game from escalating into a fight.

established pet is otherwise likely to view the newcomer as an interloper, and may attack it. Therefore, introduce them on neutral ground, in a park for example, and then walk them home together. It is not advisable to place both dogs together in the back of a car unless they are well acquainted. Otherwise they may start to fight, with potentially serious consequences.

Equipping your puppy

A new pet is most likely to stray when out for a walk, for example, and will be less inclined to return to you. This is why, at first, it is not a good idea to allow the dog to roam off its leash.

A puppy should also be fitted with a collar and you can begin training at an early stage, even before the age of three months, when the initial vaccinations will be completed. When purchasing a collar for your puppy, bear in mind that its neck will expand and buy one which allows for its growth. Check the collar regularly as well, to ensure that it is not becoming too tight.

In the case of an older dog that is used to going out for walks, it is vital to fit a collar with a medallion or capsule giving your address or telephone number.

It is also useful to buy a leash to match the collar at the same time. You may prefer a colorful nylon leash, although more traditional leather collars and leashes are equally durable. For leash-training, and for exercising an adult dog that cannot be allowed to run free, an extensible leash is a good idea. It can be played out, giving the dog freedom to roam without the risk of it disappearing too far.

TRAINING &

EXERCISE

Within a wolf pack, the young cubs learn the vital skills necessary for survival, often in inhospitable terrain, by following the example of the older members of the pack. As domestication has proceeded, so this characteristic has been emphasized by selective breeding, with puppies learning readily from their trainers. The training process itself actually serves to strengthen the bond between dog and owner, much as it helps to maintain the social fabric within the wolf pack. The training responses of certain groups of domestic dog have become more highly developed than others. This is apparent especially in gundogs that are used to working on a one-to-one basis with people, compared with pack hounds that are more independent by nature.

TRAINING
First steps

Training may sometimes be regarded as a rather one-sided activity, with the owner imposing their will on their dog, but in fact, the reason that dogs can be trained so successfully stems largely from the social structure present in the wolf pack. Domestication has simply served to refine the submissive behavior of the dog within a different hierarchy.

Young puppies like this English springer spaniel will be keen to learn, but bear in mind that they have a relatively short attention span. Short sessions are therefore recommended.

Sound training is actually of benefit to dogs themselves. A well-trained dog will not simply run away into the distance when first let off the leash. It will stay when told, which means that its owner can ensure as far as possible that potentially dangerous situations, such as a road with fast-moving traffic, are avoided. In the home itself, a dog which is house-broken and responds readily will also be a much more amenable companion.

House-training
Dogs of all ages respond best to a routine, such as the wolf establishes in the wild, seeking food and resting during certain parts of the day. Start by feeding the puppy regularly at approximately the same times every day. Then start toilet-training by placing the puppy in the required spot in the garden. It helps if this is a tiled area that can be cleaned and disinfected quite easily. Eating stimulates movement in the puppy's digestive tract, so after a meal is the time that it is most likely to want to relieve itself.

Dogs are naturally clean animals and the puppy will soon learn what is expected of it, and before long, it will return to use this spot regularly, just like wild dogs. The Southeast Asian dhole, which lives in packs like the grey wolf, even has specific, so-called "dunging sites", used by all members of the pack and located some distance from their burrows, which are never soiled.

Care outdoors
At first, always stay with your puppy in the garden, to ensure that it comes to no harm. It could encounter problems, for example if it fell into a fish pond with steep sides, although dogs can swim quite efficiently. In any event, you should check the perimeter of the garden very

Practical Pointer
Check-chains are a popular training aid to stop dogs pulling on the leash, but they must be used correctly or they can cause injury. Remove your dog's usual collar and then fit the check-chain in such a way that it slackens when pressure is relaxed. The dog should respond to the tightening of the chain by not pulling ahead or walking more slowly.

carefully for any gaps or weakness in the fences. It only needs a relatively small gap for a puppy to escape, basically one that is equivalent to the height of its body. Puppies can crouch down on all fours in order to slip under a fence or gate. All such potential exits need to be securely blocked off in advance because, once a puppy does discover a route out of the garden, it will often continue to slip out at this point, possibly with fatal consequences.

It is important to keep a watch on your puppy to prevent it from getting into trouble. Try not to leave it unsupervized, particularly out-of-doors, as it may soon become bored on its own.

Practical Pointer

Puppies can usually start to attend training classes once they are about six months old. Details of local courses can be found through your veterinarian, or possibly at your neighborhood library. Having mastered the basics, there are also advanced classes which you can participate in with your dog.

It is equally important, as a precautionary measure, to insure your puppy or dog from the outset, not only to guard against unexpected health costs, but also for public liability cover, in case your pet runs off and causes an accident.

Importance of regular training

Start carrying out regular training exercises by encouraging your puppy to walk properly on its leash. In the first instance, this can be accomplished by effectively sandwiching the dog between your left side and a wall or fence, thus encouraging your pet to walk in a straight line. Almost inevitably it will start to pull ahead, at which point you should give a quick pull on the leash and the command "heel", but pause to ensure that the puppy adopts the correct position before continuing the session.

Puppies are naturally enthusiastic, so try and use this energy in a positive way by making training an extension of play and keeping the sessions relatively short. A maximum of perhaps ten minutes tuition time will be adequate, and several lessons given through the day are usually better than one marathon course.

Puppies will learn the command to sit quite readily, since they will naturally adopt this posture. You can teach it either in conjunction with leash training or prior to a meal. If the puppy does not respond as required, then apply gentle pressure to the hindquarters as shown in the top photograph. The puppy should then stay in this position for a period of time. Always make training a positive process, and never forget to praise the puppy when it responds as required.

Puppies are a similar size at birth, with larger breeds such as this great dane then growing more rapidly than smaller breeds. Don't over-exercise the bigger breeds especially, as this can cause permanent harm.

Discipline

Training needs to be a positive experience for your dog in order to encourage it to respond in the desired way. However, there will be times when you are unhappy with its behavior, and have to resort to scolding it. In fact, the voice is one of the most potent tools in the trainer's repertoire, rather like the growling threat of the dominant wolf. The puppy will accept the scolding and register your displeasure by dropping its ears and adopting a hangdog look.

Coping with soiling

Nevertheless, there may be occasions when a scolding is likely to have very little effect, no matter how annoyed you may be. This applies particularly when the puppy has soiled in the home — rubbing its nose in the soiled carpet will actually serve no useful purpose, any more than shouting at your pet. It will simply not understand the cause of your anger unless you actually catch it in the act.

This is one situation which can be dealt with far more effectively by prevention. Try to anticipate when your puppy is likely to want to relieve itself and place it outside at these times. It is likely to take at least six months before the young dog will ask to go out of its own accord.

There may be a particular difficulty when the puppy does soil in the home because, as with wild dogs, it will be attracted back to the same spot by the scent. Apart from obviously cleaning up thoroughly and disinfecting the whole area, it is therefore advisable to use a de-scenting preparation too.

If you are going out and suspect that you may be delayed, and that your puppy may need to relieve itself, confine the young dog to part of the house, such as the bathroom, where it will be possible to clean up easily. As well as leaving its bed and a water bowl, cover the floor area for some distance around them with layers of old newspaper. With luck, if your puppy cannot wait until your return, it will use these sheets, which will absorb its urine.

Discouraging bad habits

The excitement of a puppy greeting your return is likely to result in it jumping up at you. This may not be a particular problem at this stage,

Practical Pointer

Always praise your dog when it responds as required, but do not give it an item of food on every occasion, otherwise this is likely to become a habit. When you do give a reward, a small piece of fresh carrot will be a healthy treat.

Once a dog will sit readily, it can be persuaded to offer its paw in this way without great difficulty. Training can be viewed as a progression through different steps.

Within the framework of a game, one individual is likely to be dominant to the other, as can be seen with these Dobermans. The dominant individual is climbing up on the back of the other.

although its claws could scratch you, but a large adult dog behaving in this way could easily knock over a child. It is therefore vital to establish acceptable patterns of behavior from the outset — bad habits, once acquired, will be much harder to eliminate later in life. This also calls for consistency in your approach. It is not fair to encourage your puppy onto furniture alongside you, or to let it sleep on your bed, if you then want it to desist from behaving in this way in the future.

In terms of preventing your dog from jumping up, which is a natural display of exuberance seen in wolves and other wild dogs, you must therefore encourage it to sit. This command is one of the most important and yet easily taught because dogs will sit readily. This command should be given in any situation where your dog could become over-excited and misbehave.

BASIC INSTINCTS • Pack commands

One reason dogs can be trained is due to their wolf ancestors who had to learn and follow strict rules within the wolf pack. It is the trainer who assumes the dominant role, with the dog learning to fit within the hierarchy and respond as required. It can be more effective to shake a puppy on the ground gently by the loose skin at the back of its neck, rather than resort to any other form of punishment if it is caught misbehaving.

Territories and vaccinations

Since dogs, unlike wolves, tend to live singly rather than in packs, they do not establish such strong territories. Territories not only provide security in the sense of ensuring access to prey, but they can also serve as a barrier to disease. There is no such security available to domestic dogs, especially those living at relatively high densities in urban areas. Diseases can be spread rapidly in parks and similar localities where dogs are exercised and strays may be present.

Danger of disease

Before allowing your puppy out onto the street therefore, it is vital that it is fully protected against the killer diseases which may affect dogs. Puppies frequently receive their first vaccinations at about eight weeks old, although this will not actually guarantee them complete

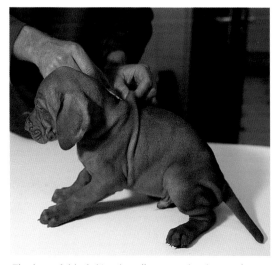

The loose fold of skin also allows vaccinations to be given without upsetting the puppy in many cases. Protection against the killer diseases such as distemper must be maintained, even if they appear to be less common than in the past.

protection. Therefore a second course is usually given when the puppies are twelve weeks old. Then annual boosters will be necessary throughout the dog's life. It is very important to maintain the protection through into old age, because the dog's ability to fight infections may decline in later life.

Your veterinarian will provide you with a vaccination certificate, which should be kept in a safe place along with other household papers. You are likely to need it if you book your dog into boarding kennels, and if you register for dog-training classes. Apart from offering the opportunity to ensure that your dog is well trained, these classes will also give your pet an opportunity to socialize with

Training should first be carried out in a yard or a quiet locality where there are no obvious distractions nearby. This will ensure that you can hold your dog's attention. Only once the basic lessons have been mastered should your pet be exercised off the leash.

other dogs. This can be important, especially for a puppy which is living on its own. It means that it is less likely to react adversely when, for example, encountering another dog while out for a walk.

Training out of the home

Having mastered the basics of training within the confines of the home and garden, you will reach the point when it will be necessary to repeat these lessons with your puppy in a strange environment. Try and choose a quiet spot for this purpose, away from any roads, other dogs, and any farm animals. Do not be surprised if, at first, your dog does not respond as you had hoped in these strange surroundings. There will inevitably be a lot of exciting distractions for the dog in the environment, such as interesting scents and unfamiliar noises.

It can be of help to have a friend or family member with you at this stage, particularly when you call your dog to you. At first though, keep the dog on an extendible leash — otherwise its curiosity will almost inevitably mean that it will run off rather than to you.

An extendible leash is a very useful training device, until you are sure that your dog will behave properly, and not seek to run off. It provides plenty of training opportunities. You can play out the leash for example, and then ask your dog to sit and stay, walking toward it rewinding the leash at this stage.

Ask the other person to hold the leash, having extended it to its maximum distance, and ensure that your dog sits with him or her. Then walk away and call the dog to you. It should then run to you, although its attention may be diverted elsewhere at first.

If you continue to use the same location for training purposes, you will ultimately be able to let your dog off the leash there, repeating the exercises which you have previously taught it. Sound pleased and enthusiastic, and always encourage your pet with plenty of praise when it responds as required.

EXERCISE
Dangers of taking your dog out

Once your dog is well trained, you can allow it much greater freedom when out walking, although try to avoid letting it stray out of sight. Otherwise it could encounter difficulties without you being aware of the situation.

Two hounds from Africa — a basenji (left) and an azawakh (right) — meet for the first time. In most cases, such encounters pass off without problems, but on occasions, displays of aggression do occur, and you should be alert to this possibility.

The lost dog
If your dog does disappear, with no indication of where it could have gone, and fails to respond to your calls, stay in the general vicinity of where you last saw it, for perhaps ten minutes or so, before retracing your steps. If you have driven to the area, you may actually find that your pet is back at the car waiting for you.

If this turns out not to be the case, report your loss to the police and to any local animal welfare organizations without delay. You can also advertize in shop windows and in local newspapers, while some radio stations also run slots for lost and found pets. You should also return with friends to search the area where your pet disappeared.

It can help to have a mobile telephone with you when walking your dog, especially if you intend to venture off a main track along woodland paths. Should an accident befall you or your pet, you can then obtain assistance without delay.

Poisonous snakes
In many areas, although not particularly common, there are poisonous snakes, which can represent a hazard to dogs, especially puppies. Puppies lack the caution of older dogs,

and can end up receiving a fatal bite as a consequence. If you suspect your pet has been bitten by a snake, try to prevent the poison becoming widely circulated into the dog's body by applying a tourniquet to the limb, above the bite, making sure that it is not too tight. The feet or the legs are the most likely areas of the body to be bitten — the situation will be much more severe if the face is attacked.

The fur around the bite is likely to appear slightly moist, while the puncture holes made

Practical Pointer
Buy a safe toy for your dog to retrieve when you are out walking, such as a flying disk, rather than simply throwing a stick for it. Otherwise this could cause injury if it hits your pet in the face.

Practical Pointer

Avoid areas where there could be hidden dangers lurking, such as sinkholes or disused mineshafts, when exercising your dog. It is also a good idea to keep your dog on its leash when taking a clifftop route.

by the snake's fangs will be apparent on closer inspection. If you hear the puppy yelp, and are close enough to see the snake, try to identify it, or at least write down a description, so that your veterinarian will be able to treat the poison appropriately. This is especially important in areas where there may be more than one species of venomous snake.

Ice and water

At certain times of the year, some routes may become more hazardous for dog-walking than others, particularly those close to water. In fact, with a young dog, it is a good idea to avoid these if possible, in case it falls in. Ice on the surface during the winter can be equally hazardous, although the weight of a dog, with its four legs, will be more evenly distributed than in our case.

Scent marking with urine is very common in dogs, especially males. They will regularly lift one of their hind legs as shown here to leave their scent in prominent localities, such as lampposts. It is also possible for urine-borne diseases to be acquired from such activities, and by sniffing, so this should be discouraged as far as possible.

Never be tempted to follow your dog across ice, because it could easily give way, plunging both you and your pet into the chilly water beneath. Ironically, your dog is more likely than you to survive this experience, because its thick coat will help to insulate it from the cold, and it may also find it easier to clamber out onto the bank again.

Coast and clifftop

On the coast, try to avoid allowing your dog to wander along a pier head, or groyne, when it is off the leash, because it could lose its footing, especially if the surface is slippery, and it might end up being swept out to sea by the current. If you do take your dog on the beach, be sure that it does not upset fellow beach-users, and take a bottle and bowl so that it can drink fresh water if it becomes thirsty.

Some dogs are naturally better swimmers than others, but always be careful, especially if your dog goes into the sea, as currents can be dangerous.

COMMUNICA

TION & BEHAVIOR

Dogs communicate in similar ways to wolves, although they rely more strongly on vocalizations, whereas wolves are shyer and more reluctant to reveal their position by this means. Scent marking is very important for both wolves and dogs. Urine serves as an indicator of the dog's social ranking, and is an individual marker that males deposit as an indicator of their presence, on lampposts, trees or similarly prominent sites where other canids are likely to be passing.

When dogs or wolves meet, their body language will provide subtle clues to whether the encounter will prove friendly or is likely to lead to aggression. Dogs use a clearly defined series of gestures of increasing intensity that are normally employed as a deterrent before violence results. This serves to defuse conflicts without the risk of physical injury.

COMMUNICATION
Barking

Members of the wolf pack keep in touch with each other by howling. Their baying call echoes across the landscape, but the risk is that the wolves may reveal their positions not only to fellow pack members, but also to members of neighboring packs, which may be seeking to invade their territory. As a result, wolves will not always acknowledge the calls of their neighbors.

The sound of wolves howling at night can be very eerie, with their calls being audible over long distances.

In the case of dogs, their ability to sense danger and to indicate the threat by barking was clearly of great value right from the outset of the domestication process. Just the barking of a dog could be sufficient to deter a potential aggressor or would-be thief. Barking, as distinct from howling, became a positive trait which was actively encouraged by those owning dogs.

At close quarters, a dog will rely on its sight to locate its owner. Domestic dogs tend to be noisier than wolves, barking intently if they detect strangers or any possible danger. More casual barking may relate to a cat in the vicinity.

Different-sounding barks
Today, the sound of a dog's bark differs, according to the breed. Howling remains a feature typically associated with those breeds from northern latitudes, which remain most closely allied to wolves in terms of their appearance. This so-called "sled-dog" group, as exemplified by the Siberian husky, will engage in communal howling, just like wolves. They only call in this way when standing still.

Many hounds have a baying call, which is used to keep in contact with other members of the pack, when they are in undergrowth for example, and also when they are following a scent. The sound of the bark is not necessarily a reflection of the size of the dog concerned, however, as some small breeds, such as the Cavalier King Charles spaniel, have a relatively deep bark suggestive of a much larger dog. In fact, some of the smaller dogs often rank among the most noisy.

Control of barking

It is possible to teach dogs not to bark, or even to operate on them for this purpose, as happened in northern Europe during the First World War. At this time, many dogs were used as messengers in the trenches, and barking for any reason could have had very serious consequences for all concerned.

In those situations where barking may be desirable, alerting you to someone at the door perhaps, it is equally important to encourage your dog to stop once you are aware of the situation. Puppies should be trained to be quiet at this point, rather than being allowed to continue barking.

This behavior is often caused by excitement, so it is important to keep the young dog calm, rather than allowing it to become overexcited, at the prospect of a visitor for example. Barking begins early in puppyhood, starting when dogs are as young as three weeks old.

Barking difficulties

Today, barking can create problems under certain circumstances. Dogs may become conditioned to bark, as the result of their owner going out for example, and this can be very disturbing, particularly for close neighbors, and often leads to complaints and ill-feeling. Described as "separation anxiety", this problem is most likely to arise in the case of dogs that have spent part of their lives in kennels.

When you need to leave your dog on its own, be sure to exercise it first, allowing it a good run off the leash. This may encourage it to sleep rather than pine in your absence. Leaving the radio on may also be helpful.

Separation anxiety

Like many such behavioral difficulties, this can usually be overcome with patience, provided that the owner is aware of this situation. Always remember that the dog is behaving in this way because it is very distressed and agitated. Dogs do still retain the pack instinct of the wolf, although this trait may be more apparent in the case of certain breeds, such as hounds, than in others.

The dog relates to its owner as a pack member and so it barks when it is left in apparent isolation, uncertain as to when, or if, its owner will return. At the sound of its owner's footsteps or voice, such behavior is likely to cease because its cause is removed.

Actual treatment of separation anxiety depends on you going out of your home for variable periods of time, typically between five minutes and half an hour, although you will need to stay within earshot. If your dog barks, and possibly scratches at the door as well, ignore it when you go back into the home. Only praise your pet if it has not barked while you have been out.

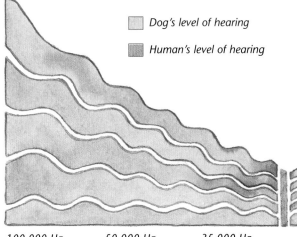

Dog's level of hearing

Human's level of hearing

100,000 Hz   50,000 Hz   35,000 Hz   20 Hz

Dogs have a much better sense of hearing than ourselves, being able to detect sounds at higher frequency, and so they can pick up sounds which are quite inaudible to our ears.

Domestic dogs seek to establish and mark territories just like wolves, although their instincts in this respect are generally not as strong. This may be related in part to the fact that many dogs live alone, rather than in packs.

Scent

Dogs rely heavily on scent-marking as a means of indicating their presence in an area, much as a pack of wolves will signal the borders of their territory. This will be particularly noticeable if you take your dog on the same route each time that you go out for a walk. It will pause to sniff at the same sites, such as tree stumps and posts for example, with male dogs in particular often urinating on the site afterwards.

Male dogs are far more likely to scent-mark in this way, cocking one of their hind legs for this purpose. Interestingly, puppies of both sexes will keep their feet on the ground when urinating, rather like a bitch, until sexual maturity is attained and this distinction becomes evident. Raising its leg allows the male dog to direct its urine more accurately – some dogs will urinate with either leg raised off the ground, whereas others show a distinct preference for one particular leg.

The volume of urine that is passed at each of these localities is often quite small, with males typically urinating about three times more frequently than bitches when out on a walk. Areas that are commonly passed by dogs, such as lampposts, are most likely to be sprayed in this fashion, because the scent of other dogs will encourage your dog to leave its mark as well.

In contrast to more solitary members of the dog family, the domestic dog produces a urine which has far less of an odor than that of foxes, for example, but it still contains pheromones – chemical messengers which can be spread on the air currents, with the scent being picked up by other dogs.

Dogs rely on a special adaption of their nasal pathway to help detect this scent. Located in the roof of their mouth, they have a so-called "vomeronasal organ", also known as Jacobsen's organ. Air containing scent molecules can be detected by this organ, which is connected by a neural pathway to the medial parts of the hypothalamus and preoptic area of the brain. This part of the brain is more concerned with sexual activity than feeding behavior.

After urinating as a means of scent-marking, a male dog may also scratch the ground, if it is earth or something similar. This provides further evidence of its territorial claim by giving a visual indication as well. Glands between the toes may also leave a further deposit of scent when the dog does this.

It is not uncommon, if you decide to take on another dog, for your established pet to display what may appear to be a breakdown in its toilet-training, but this is actually a means of trying to assert its continued dominance in the home. This phase will generally pass once the

Practical Pointer

Dogs have no difficulty in locating food concealed out of sight, for example in a bag left on the kitchen floor. You may then come home to find the bag ripped apart, and the food consumed. Therefore avoid leaving food within easy reach, even if it is hidden.

dogs become better acquainted, although you may have to consider neutering if all else fails.

The ability of the dog to detect scents is not a constant feature, but it is influenced by various factors. A hungry dog, for example, is likely to be able to track far more effectively than one which has just been fed. Although it is often said that a dry nose is a sign of illness in a dog, this is not necessarily the case, but a dry nose will depress its scenting skills. The moisture inhaled along with the molecules of scent aids the dog's scent detection.

BASIC INSTINCTS • Scent marking

Male wolves behave in a similar way to dogs, scent-marking trees, for example, within their territorial boundaries. They constantly use the same localities, so the wolf or dog is able to reinforce its presence in the area. The ability to cock the leg is important, because otherwise, male dogs would have great difficulty in directing their urine. Bitches, like puppies of both sexes, will squat when urinating. Their urine tends to be more acidic, and it can lead to dead patches of grass developing on a lawn over a period of time.

Practical Pointer

Apart from pheromones, a number of potentially serious diseases can be spread via dog's urine, which is why it is so important to keep vaccinations up to date.

Some dogs have a much more acute sense of smell than others, with the bloodhound being one of the most effective trackers in the world. They can follow scents which were made days earlier.

The surface of the leathery tip of a dog's nose, encompassing the nostrils, is kept moist by means of the nasal lachrymal duct, which acts as a conduit, enabling tear fluid to drain down the nose. The flexible nature of the nostrils also means that they can be flared, which may help them to capture more scent molecules as the dog sniffs.

BEHAVIOR
Contact with other dogs

Two dogs meeting when out for a walk are likely to be slightly wary of each other. They will probably circle around, sniffing cautiously at each other's hindquarters. Size is not necessarily a reliable indication of which dog may prove to be the dominant individual, as a small dog will not necessarily be intimidated by a larger rival.

You may actually miss the key moment which will probably determine the order of dominance, because it is not obvious. When the dogs sniff noses, they also stare at each other — the one which looks away first will be the submissive individual.

Age also plays a part in seniority, just as it does in wolf packs. Recently weaned puppies

When one dog encounters another, it may respond by raising its hackles — the fur at the back of the neck, as in the top photograph. This does not mean fighting is inevitable.

will inevitably have a lower social ranking than an older dog, which is why it is usually easier to introduce a puppy rather than a middle-aged dog alongside an established individual.

The subordinate dog will react by cowering if threatened, while the dominant individual may place its paw on the other dog's back, depending on their relative sizes, and keep its tail erect. The encounter is likely to end with the weaker dog retreating back to its owner. There is rarely any conflict under these circumstances if the owners are in the vicinity.

However, a dangerous situation may arise in the case of ex-racing greyhounds. Once their track careers are over, these athletic hounds can make excellent pets as they have extremely gentle natures. Nevertheless, greyhounds have been trained to pursue a toy hare, and when out walking, they are liable to react to small dogs, such as Yorkshire terriers, in a similar way, except that the smaller dog may be seized and killed. For this reason, always ensure that a greyhound is muzzled when off the leash. Its sheer pace means that, if it spots a small dog in the distance, you will have no hope of catching it in time to prevent an attack.

Contact with cats

Although dogs are often ready to chase any cats which cross their path, it is usual for a cat living in a home with a dog to be the dominant individual. This is often a lesson which puppies need to learn. If cornered, the cat is likely to stand its ground and hiss loudly. If this is not a sufficient deterrent, the cat will be prepared to use its claws in order to stop the puppy's advances.

In such cases, the puppy is unlikely to display the behavior typical of a subordinate, but will simply withdraw, taking care to avoid coming into direct contact with the cat in the future. The one situation where your dog may

Unusual friendships can form between dogs and cats. This bonding is most likely when the animals have grown up together and the dog's social instincts have been directed toward its companion.

respond aggressively, however, is if the cat tries to steal its food. As a precaution, be sure to exclude the cat when feeding your dog.

Contact with other pets

It is also not a good idea to allow your dog any opportunity of coming into direct contact with small pets, particularly rabbits, which are the natural quarry of many breeds. Terriers, for example, will instinctively kill rats, while hounds will often pursue rabbits. Even a tame dog may instinctively respond in this way, particularly when the other animal moves, hopping off in the case of a rabbit. Unlike a cat, these creatures have no way of defending themselves if cornered.

Practical Pointer
If your dog is scratched or even bitten by a cat, be sure to wash the wound without delay, using an antiseptic solution. Otherwise, particularly following a bite, an infection may develop at the site because of the unpleasant bacteria in the cat's mouth.

Opposite *Two wolves fighting. Here the contest is virtually over, with the weaker individual on its back. It will get back on its feet and run off, probably being pursued for a short distance by its opponent.*

Signs of aggression

Over the centuries following the start of the domestication process, the dog has spent so much time with humans that it regards people with whom it has regular contact in the same way as pack members. The dog has developed body language to communicate with humans and has lost some of its ability to establish bonds with its own kind. This is a reflection of the fact that, in many cases, dogs are tending to live more solitary lives, isolated from their own kind for much of the day, apart from when they are out walking.

Practical Pointer

Disputes between dogs may arise not just over food. Playthings can also provide a source of conflict. Offering a choice should help to prevent any serious aggression arising, although dogs that know each other well may play with a toy together.

Serious combat between two wolves. Contests are most likely to be bloody when the leader of the pack is challenged by a subordinate. The opponents are likely to be well-matched, with neither backing down readily.

Fighting instincts

Selective breeding has also played a part, and in some cases, the dog's natural territorial and aggressive tendencies toward its fellows have been deliberately reinforced. This was undertaken to create breeds, such as the Staffordshire bull terrier, for use in dogfighting. In spite of the fact that breeders have worked hard to eliminate aggressive traits from this and other similar breeds today, such dogs can still, on occasions, be very unpredictable in the company of others.

The actual appearance of breeds that are bred for dogfighting is similar, for practical reasons. They all have a relatively short, square, powerful muzzle, which enables them to exert a strong bite and take a firm grip on their opponent. Their eyes are relatively small and deeply set to protect against injury, while the skin on their necks is quite loose, so that a bite here is more likely to result in a superficial rather than a deep injury.

Pack behavior

In contrast, the situation with pack dogs is markedly different. This is not to say that they always agree, particularly in the case of sled dogs, which retain the closest resemblance to wolves. Arguments over dominance are not uncommon among this group — each team has its canine leader, and especially with new dogs, it will take time for the social order to become established.

But they will then bond and work as a team, which serves to reinforce the pack instinct between them, preventing disputes at this stage in the same way that wolves will not fight when hunting together. It is highly unlikely that wolves would have become such successful predators if their ability to cooperate had not evolved. A single wolf, on its own, is virtually unable to tackle large and dangerous prey, such as moose. The availability of prey is one of the main influences on pack size.

Cooperative hunting is a feature of many hound breeds, such as beagles and bassets. The social nature of dogs is one of the reasons why they have proved to be such popular companions, as they see the family as a pack, and adopt a subordinate role in the group.

Pack hounds, in spite of the fact that they were originally developed for hunting prey, are actually very friendly, genial dogs by nature. If you are seeking two dogs which will live in relative harmony with each other, choosing from this group of breeds is recommended.

Pack rivalry within a group of hounds. Fighting is much more common among male rather than female dogs.

Although they are not generally aggressive, ex-racing greyhounds in particular should be muzzled when walking in parks and other places where they could encounter small dogs. The greyhound may otherwise chase and catch its smaller relative.

Practical Pointer

Adult dogs are often far more tolerant of the attentions of puppies than of another adult dog, because they are perceived in a different way – not as rivals, but rather as natural subordinates. Maintain this situation by not favoring the puppy in the presence of the older dog.

The fear factor

When purchasing a puppy it is virtually impossible to tell whether or not an individual will prove aggressive later in life, especially since this will depend in part on how the dog is reared. Much will also depend on its environment and particularly its training, although, especially in the case of bigger dogs, males are likely to be more dominant than females.

Levels of aggression

The overall level of aggression in a wolf pack, even among cubs, starts to rise during the winter period. Male cubs will often begin to build up a dominance over their female siblings, based in part on their larger size. Soon they will start interacting increasingly with the pack members of lower rank, and gradually start to establish a place for themselves in the hierarchy. This change in behavior becomes apparent once the young

A child brought up with dogs is unlikely to be afraid of them in later life. Young children see their dogs as both friends and protectors. However, always supervize contact between them — dogs are not toys!

Some breeds have acquired a reputation for aggression, which may be heightened by their appearance. Ear cropping is outlawed in many countries, but it serves to give breeds, such as this Doberman, a fiercer appearance with its ears raised.

wolves are two years old, by which time they are also becoming increasingly aggressive.

With naturally assertive breeds of domestic dog, such as the rottweiler or the Doberman, problems are therefore most likely to develop not in puppyhood, but from two years of age onward. This is why firm training from an early age is so important, so that dogs do not start to challenge their owners, or other members of the family, at this critical later stage in their lives.

Fear of dogs

Some people are fearful of dogs, and this is something which a dog will be able to detect and interpret as a sign of submission. The temperament of domestic dogs is, however, far more stable than that of wolves. Certain breeds, notably those of the toy group, have in fact been specifically bred as companions. Not surprisingly therefore, these are the most suitable breeds as family pets.

It tends to be breeds that most closely resemble the wolf in terms of their appearance, such as the German shepherd dog, which inspire the greatest fear. Human antipathy toward the wolf is very deep-seated, and probably dates back to the time when people were switching from a nomadic, hunting life style to a pastoral existence.

Flock guardians

Wolf packs would have represented a serious threat to herds of sheep and goats in particular, at a time long before the development of firearms. Up until this stage, apart from the alertness of those watching over the animals, the main defense was by means of the wolf's domestic relative, in the form of flock guardians such as the Maremma sheepdog in Italy, or the komondor in Hungary.

Other, similar types of dog were developed throughout Europe. They tended to be whitish in color, as this helped them to blend in among the flocks that they were protecting. It also served to distinguish them readily at a distance from the dark-colored wolf.

Additional protection for these large dogs was provided by large, spiked collars, which guarded the vulnerable area of their throat. However, since the demise of the wolf during the late nineteenth and twentieth centuries in this part of the world, these flock guardians have become much scarcer, although some are now being seen in the show ring with increasing frequency.

Practical Pointer

Delve into the history of any breed which appeals to you before making a final decision about which to choose. This will give you a clear insight into a dog's likely temperament. Dogs evolved for guarding purposes are most likely to display aggression toward their owners and other people.

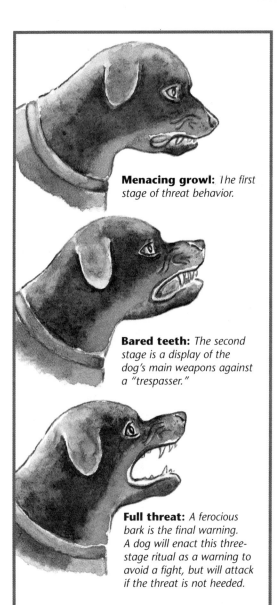

Menacing growl: *The first stage of threat behavior.*

Bared teeth: *The second stage is a display of the dog's main weapons against a "trespasser."*

Full threat: *A ferocious bark is the final warning. A dog will enact this three-stage ritual as a warning to avoid a fight, but will attack if the threat is not heeded.*

SIGNS OF DANGER

The body language of dogs is very important, particularly because a dog will usually make a series of gestures before, for example, attempting to bite. If these are not detected by a young child, the outcome could be serious, with the child possibly being badly injured as a result. Never leave a child alone with a dog. It is not just coincidence that children are more likely to be bitten than adults. They may also play more roughly with the dog, pulling its tail for example, and be less aware of the warning signs.

Lips drawn back with the canines exposed is a clear warning sign that this dog will attack if challenged any further. It will also be giving a menacing growl. Dogs rarely launch into a sudden attack, but display a series of signs of increasing aggression.

Displays of territorial aggression are similar, although the dog may not bite as readily as when it is in pain. Barking is also more common in such cases, providing a means of deterring the intruder without having to resort to physical violence.

Effect of past experience

Past experiences may also exert an effect on the dog's reactions. If it has been repeatedly teased for example, then, as a result, it may be more likely to bite with less warning. One of the potential difficulties with rescued dogs is that you cannot be sure of their previous experiences, with the result that something

Avoid taking on an adult dog if you have a young family, unless you know the dog's history in detail. It may have been rehomed because of its aggressive tendencies, although the animal shelter may not have been told this by the previous owner. Regaining the confidence of a mistreated dog can also be difficult.

Aggression toward people

Dogs rarely bite without some provocation, although some breeds are potentially more aggressive than others, because they will not accept a subservient role, and so are more likely to challenge younger family members in particular. Dominant breeds of this type include the rottweiler and other large dogs that are used as guardians.

A dog will often display its aggression by raising its hackles – the area of fur at the base of the neck – and drawing back its lips to reveal its canine teeth. This is often accompanied by growling, while at the same time, the dog will keep its tail raised. If these signs are ignored, then the teeth will be fully exposed before the dog launches into an attack.

Practical Pointer

It is not just in the home that dogs can display territorial instincts. They may behave in a similar way if they are left in a car. This behavior is especially likely to arise if passers-by have teased your dog in the past by banging on a window. In any event, avoid leaving a dog in a car when the weather is very warm, because of the risk of heatstroke.

from their past, even as simple as a particular color or style of coat, may cause them to display signs of aggression and start to growl.

Try to isolate the cause under these circumstances, and never force the dog to confront the situation directly, because this is highly likely to result in its becoming more and more distressed and aggressive. In this case, you should seek the advice of a behavioral consultant to address the problem and, in due course, perhaps overcome your dog's fear.

Below *There are times when aggression in a dog is required by its handler, as here in the case of a police dog that is being trained to apprehend a fleeing criminal. The dog is taught to seize the lower part of the arm, and not to inflict any serious injury.*

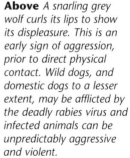

Above *A snarling grey wolf curls its lips to show its displeasure. This is an early sign of aggression, prior to direct physical contact. Wild dogs, and domestic dogs to a lesser extent, may be afflicted by the deadly rabies virus and infected animals can be unpredictably aggressive and violent.*

Playtime

Dogs are naturally playful from puppyhood onwards, although, with advancing age, they often become less inclined to use toys. Play has important social implications for dogs, helping to establish their social ranking at a relatively early age, as happens with wolf cubs. It can help to avoid the need for fighting, by testing their strength without overt signs of conflict. Dogs will very rarely injure each other during the course of a game.

One of the most distinctive indicators of a dog's desire to play is the so-called "play bow." The dog crouches down on its front legs and, if ignored at this stage, may bark excitedly to attract attention. It then bounces up and may run off for a short distance before repeating this performance should there be no obvious reaction from the other dog or its owner.

When playing together, dogs will often tend to jump and bounce, rather than walking normally. They may chase after each other and rear up on their hind legs, pawing at each other with their front legs. Small dogs tend to be more playful by nature than their larger relatives, with poodles, for example, often being great clowns. They often circle tightly and ultimately one may roll over on its back. This is a gesture of submission, also seen as a sign of surrender in a fight, but in this case, the body language is decidedly different. Instead of avoiding eye contact, as in the case of a fight, the dog on the ground will continue staring at its companion and will not fold back its ears as a gesture of appeasement.

Toys

Play between an owner and a dog is equally important as a means of reinforcing the bonding process. An ever-increasing range of toys for this purpose can be found in pet stores. They can be broadly divided into three categories. The first includes toys such as balls, which the dog can chase and retrieve. Many dogs appreciate toys of this type, although they perhaps have the strongest appeal for spaniels and retrievers, which will instinctively seek out and return with such items.

Throwing a ball for your dog to bring back to you means that your pet will get far more exercise on even a short walk than would be the case if it trotted alongside you. Special flying disks have also become popular toys for dogs —

Practical Pointer

With all toys, it is sensible to train your dog to relinquish the item on command. Otherwise you could find that the dog becomes possessive to the point where it snaps if you try to take its toy away.

This greyhound is making a "play bow" indicating that it wants to play.

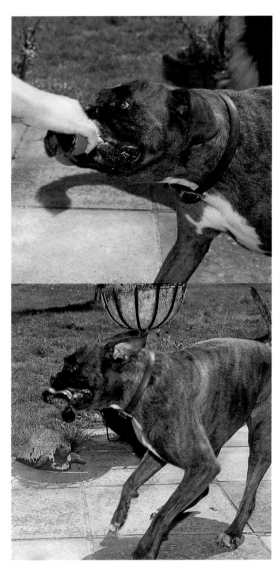

these are made with soft material which should not damage your pet's teeth, unlike those sold as children's toys or for beach use.

Second, there are chew toys, which help to keep your dog's teeth in good condition. They have largely replaced the typical marrow bones, which used to be sold for this purpose, proving to be more hygienic and less messy around the home. Domestic dogs have relatively little opportunity to exercise their teeth on bones in the same way as wolves, and so such toys can be valuable, especially for puppies during their teething phase, when they are about five months old.

Finally, pull toys are also popular with dogs, but need to be used more cautiously, especially with an older dog, whose teeth may not be in the best condition. Toys of this type may be either solid or comprised of fibers, which often tend to become rather congealed with the dog's saliva.

Flying disks are very popular with dogs, with the unpredictability of their flight adding to the excitement of the game. Choose special disks intended for dogs because they are generally made of softer material than those sold as toys. Dogs also enjoy tug toys, but it is important to ensure that your dog is trained to drop the item on command.

Practical Pointer

Only use toys which are safe for your dog to play with. It is not unknown for dogs to choke on unsuitable items used as playthings, which end up being swallowed and causing an obstruction in the throat.

Agility events such as this one at Crufts are open to dogs of all types and sizes, with the dog being judged on the time it takes to get round the course rather than on its appearance. Agility courses harness and test the natural abilities of dogs. Their trainers play a vital role in encouraging the dog.

Dog damage

Some degree of damage around the home is inevitable, particularly if you start out with a puppy. Carpets and doors are likely to bear the brunt of the puppy's attentions. By trying to anticipate its needs, however, you will be able to minimize the likelihood of any serious damage. Placing the puppy outdoors after meals, and both first thing in the morning and again at night should help to prevent soiling in the home. By dealing with antisocial behavior on the part of your puppy, you should prevent this from becoming habitual.

Conditioning can be significant in this respect. Your puppy may be in the garden and scratching at the door to be let in. If you immediately respond, you are likely to set off a cycle in which your dog scratches repeatedly at the door on every occasion when it is ready to come indoors, with its claws soon damaging the wood. Prevention in this case will depend on you anticipating how long your dog should be left outside and then calling it back inside before it becomes bored.

He may look cute but this lurcher puppy is likely to cause some damage around the home. Note the torn cloth on which he is lying — providing dogs with their own bed will help to safeguard furniture.

It starts as a desire to come in. The dog tries to push open the door but if the door is closed it may decide to scratch, and this immediately attracts your attention. A pattern of behavior may then form which can soon develop into a serious problem.

Damage in the home

Try to avoid shutting your puppy in a room, certainly on a regular basis, because here again, it will start scratching, potentially damaging both the door and carpeting. It is much better to have a special pen in which your puppy can be safely confined when it is not possible to allow it a free run around the home.

The teething phase can result in quite severe damage to furniture should your puppy seek to relieve the irritation of its developing teeth by gnawing, for example, on a table leg. You will need to keep a close watch on your puppy at

Practical Pointer

Bored dogs are more apt to become destructive. To prevent this try and provide plenty of toys and exercise for your pet.

this stage and provide a good selection of chew toys to minimize damage around the home.

If you have any particularly valuable items, perhaps within your puppy's reach, it is always a good idea to move them to another part of the house, especially since most household insurance policies will not cover you for damage of this type.

Damage in the garden

Dogs can also cause problems in the garden, often digging in flower beds and lawns. Any fertilizers applied need to be selected carefully — a dog may delight in rolling in manure, or even want to eat it. Dogs will also dig to bury food items, such as bones. This behavior mimics the way in which wolves seek to hide surplus food in the hope of returning to it and eating it at a later stage. Burying food means that it will be more likely to escape the attention of scavengers.

There is little to be gained by interfering once the hole is dug, although you may want to remove the item before it is retrieved again. Dogs will eat rotting food, and while this may not upset the digestive system of wolves, it is certainly much more likely to disturb that of their domestic relatives.

Although dogs usually prefer to dig in flower beds, where the soil is softer, and can be excavated more readily, they will equally seek to dig in a lawn if there is no other option available. Their relatively short, blunt claws are ideal for ripping through the turf and either foot may be used for digging.

Neither is it uncommon for them to forage for food in the garden. While fallen apples being used for play, and gnawed, will cause little worry, a dog which chooses to help itself to a row of carrots is unlikely to enjoy a favorable reception from the gardener in the family. Unfortunately, this type of behavior can also soon become habitual — for example, after obtaining several carrots, the dog will return in search of more. The only solution is to fence off this part of the garden to exclude the dog.

BASIC INSTINCTS • Digging

Dogs will readily dig in the garden, particularly if you have buried any edible items in a compost heap or trench for example. This can have longer term and serious consequences, should it cause the dog to fall in. This behavior originates from that of wild dogs, which use their powers of scent to locate edible items such as roots when other food may be harder to obtain, or retrieve food which they have themselves buried previously. Most wild dogs are essentially scavengers. Their adaptability and resourcefulness in obtaining food is responsible for the wide natural distribution of the family today.

Practical Pointer

If you have a male dog which suddenly digs a hole under a fence and heads out of the garden, there is probably a bitch on heat in the neighborhood.

PROBLEMS
Changing view of the dog

Nowadays, with so many distinctive breeds of domestic dog, it may be hard to imagine that, as selective breeding continues, they are still diverging further from their wild ancestor. Although breeding has already eliminated many undesirable traits that would have been apparent in the early days of domestication, such as restlessness and wariness of people, there have been distinct drawbacks, most notably in terms of the dog's physical soundness.

Physical problems

Problems such as hip dysplasia, in which the hip joints are weakened, and luxating patellas, a weakness which affects the kneecaps of smaller breeds especially, have become prominent in domestic dogs, whereas such afflictions are not encountered in the case of the wolf. Breeders are striving to eliminate such physical shortcomings from their bloodlines by careful monitoring of breeding stock.

Weaknesses affecting the skeletal system such as hip dysplasia are fairly common in dogs, and can prove a severe handicap, especially if the dog is overweight. In this case the head of the femur does not sit snugly in the socket on the hip, failing to provide proper support.

Rage syndrome

Unexpected problems do crop up on occasions, however, and can relate to temperament as much as physical soundness. One of the most worrying examples of this type is the so-called "rage syndrome", which can be found in some normally placid breeds, such as cocker spaniels and labrador retrievers. Such dogs appear normal, but suffer from uncontrollable bouts of rage. They are highly unpredictable and will attack without the usual warning signals.

The only indicator of this problem may be a glazed expression. Research has shown that there are usually distinct genetic links in such cases. Once a problem of this type has been identified, suspect or affected bloodlines should not be used for breeding purposes, and dogs suffering from the condition should be destroyed to safeguard the community.

Effects of dog shows

One of the positive aspects of the dog-show scene is that it has actually encouraged the development of those breeds with sound temperaments over the past century or so, ever since events of this type began to be held regularly. Judges will simply not give awards to dogs which show signs of aggression in the ring, either to other dogs or to people.

In fact, without the interest generated by dog shows such as Crufts and the Westminster Kennel Club Show held in New York, where a wide variety of breeds is put on view, it is possible that some might well have died out, or would have been greatly reduced in numbers.

Events such as these, where the dogs are judged to prescribed standards laid down for each breed, are different from field trials, which seek to assess the working abilities of individual dogs rather than their physical appearance. They give an opportunity for dogs to work in close association with their handlers, which is a feature further developed in the various obedience and agility competitions, often held in conjunction with regular dog shows.

The type of dog is of no significance whatsoever at such events, and in fact, it is quite common to see both cross-bred and mongrel dogs taking part. These events can show just how the pack instinct present in wolves has been transformed into a very close bond between dog and handler, enabling them to work together as a team.

Above Show dogs have to learn to be tolerant of other dogs in close proximity to them, and to accept being handled by the judge, who is likely to be a stranger, without misbehaving in any way.

Below A judge checks a wire-haired dachshund for soundness. The requirements for such dogs and points for particular features are laid down in the official breed standard. This may also list faults in some cases.

FEEDING &

HEALTH

Dogs are highly adaptable in their feeding habits, and this characteristic underlies the wide range of the wolf, as well as helping to explain why dogs were so widely kept in primitive societies. While canids were instinctively carnivorous, they are not above scavenging, and when other food is in short supply they will consume almost anything edible, including insects, berries and even plants. Living in this way does take its toll however, with wolves having a much shorter live expectancy than their domesticated relatives. Great advances in the field of canine health care, particularly for older individuals, means that dogs are now living longer than at any stage in the past. Even the large breeds, which tend to have a shorter lifespan than their smaller relatives, are in many cases now living for more than a decade.

FEEDING
Food and diet

Dogs, like wolves, prefer to feed on meat but they will eat vegetables and there are even specially formulated vegetarian diets to keep them in good health. Feeding meat is not without its dangers because, whereas a wolf has access to the whole carcass, a domestic dog only receives selected parts, such as organ meat like spleen or the stomach (sold as tripe), which by themselves do not represent a balanced diet. These are low in calcium for example, and a dog fed in this fashion will soon start to suffer from nutritional deficiencies if its diet is not supplemented.

The dog's level of activity will determine the type of food which it needs. Active dogs such as racing greyhounds require a different diet from that of a sedentary older pet. A growing range of prepared foods to meet the demands of dogs at all stages in their lives is now available.

Practical Pointer
When weighing your dog, lift it up and stand on the bathroom scales with it. Then subtract your own weight from the total to find the dog's weight.

As a result, the availability of balanced foods has helped greatly to popularize the keeping of dogs. Containing all the essential ingredients to keep dogs in good health, these foods can be used straight from the can or packet.

Canned foods
Canned foods have proved popular for many years and tend to be preferred by dogs because their relatively high water content is similar to that of meat itself. Cans are heavy to carry in quantity, however, and any of their contents left uneaten will have to be stored in a refrigerator to prevent them deteriorating or attracting flies. Special plastic covers can be obtained for this purpose, which also prevent the odor of the food permeating into the surrounding air.

Dry foods
Dry foods for dogs are now very popular. They offer a more concentrated ration than canned food, and, because of their low water content, they do not require any special storage conditions, other than being kept dry. Take care to follow the instructions regarding the amount of food required, however, because if you persist in offering an excess, your dog will soon show signs of obesity.

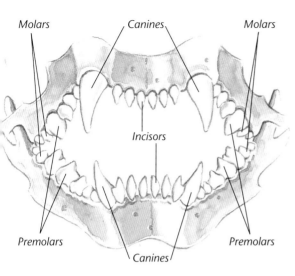

Molars   Canines   Molars

Incisors

Premolars   Premolars

Canines

The dentition of the dog. It shows the typical pattern of a carnivore, with the prominent canine teeth, used to kill prey, clearly visible at the corners of the mouth, with the incisors at the front often serving to seize prey in the first instance.

The use of dry foods can be especially recommended for breeds such as poodles, which may suffer badly from dental decay and gum disease, because such foods help to keep the teeth free from the tartar that predisposes to this type of problem. A dog fed on dry food, however, will drink more than if it were eating canned food, to make up for the relative deficiency of fluid in its food.

Semi-moist foods

The third type of food now available is semi-moist, although perhaps surprisingly, it has not proved especially popular with dog owners. It retains the moist characteristic of canned food combined with the convenience and concentration of a dry food. The addition of sugar as a preservative means that it is not recommended for dogs suffering from diabetes mellitus. Semi-moist foods are sold in packets which need to be kept sealed after opening, to prevent their contents from becoming dry.

Obesity

One of the major problems in the dog world today is that an increasing number of dogs are suffering from obesity. This is something which now affects roughly thirty percent of dogs. If you are concerned about your dog's weight, you can refer in the first instance to a book which contains the breed standard — this will provide you with an indication of the normal weight for the breed. In many cases, male dogs tend to be slightly larger and heavier than bitches. With a cross-bred dog, it is obviously harder to assess its ideal weight, but if you can no longer see or feel your pet's ribs, it is almost certainly overweight.

Obesity can have a number of adverse effects on a dog's health, and is a contributory factor to heart and joint disease, as in people. Neutering, by altering the hormonal balance in the body, can also predispose to obesity, to the extent that, after such surgery, the dog's food intake may need to be reduced significantly to prevent this problem arising.

Special obesity diets are available to help in a dog's slimming program, but you should not rely on these alone. Increasing the amount of exercise will be just as significant in ensuring that your dog not only loses weight, but also stays fit. The domestic dog leads a very sedentary life compared with its ancestor, and will readily become obese as a result.

A typical range of different types of prepared foods is shown here, as well as various types of chews and treats. Be careful not to overfeed your dog, as it can rapidly become obese.

Dogs will often prefer to drink from ponds and puddles rather than from a water bowl. They rarely fall ill as a result. Try to monitor how much they are drinking because this can be crucial to their health.

Water

A supply of fresh drinking water should always be available to dogs. A water container which will not be tipped over easily should be used for this purpose, because the dog may otherwise place its foot on the rim, tipping over the container and spilling its contents.

It is also important to wash the dog's water bowl thoroughly about twice a week. Bacteria can and do develop in stale water, and could cause a digestive disturbance. Nevertheless, dogs will often prefer to drink from standing sources of water, such as ponds or puddles, just like their wild ancestor. The reason for such behavior is unclear — perhaps it is partly to do with taste — but usually, no harm will result.

Drinking while out walking

There are potential risks when your dog is out for a walk, and becomes thirsty. It is then more likely to drink contaminated water than would otherwise be the case. Be particularly careful around any farm buildings, where there could be contaminated sources of water. It is always better to take a supply of drinking water for your dog if you are going on a relatively lengthy trek, especially if the weather is hot. Special water bottles for this purpose, which will also convert into drinkers, and can be easily carried on a shoulder strap, are now available.

The situation may be worse if you are on a beach, because without a drink, your dog may resort to drinking seawater, which, with its high salt content, will worsen its thirst and could make it seriously ill. In addition, dogs may encounter difficulties if they plunge into the water in search of a drink.

Monitoring water consumption

At home, always keep a close watch on the volume of water which your dog is drinking, particularly as it gets older. Increased water consumption may be indicative of kidney failure and a number of other ailments. Do not restrict your dog's water intake under these circumstances, as this is likely to have dire results. Obviously, drinking more will result in the production of more urine, so that your dog is more likely to soil in the house as well.

This convenient drinker means that you do not have to carry a separate water bottle and bowl when you go out with your dog. It comes complete with shoulder straps as seen here.

Wolves and dogs drink in an identical fashion, lapping up water using their tongue, with the tip of the tongue expanding rather like a ladle for this purpose. Some water will inevitably be spilt, and so you should position your dog's water bowl on a non-absorbent surface. The bowl itself should also be designed so that it cannot be tipped over easily.

Practical Pointer

It is not a good idea to give dogs cow's milk to drink. Some dogs may not be able to digest it, and end up suffering from diarrhea. Stick to a dog-milk replacer, especially for puppies. This is available from pet stores and simply needs to be mixed with water.

AILMENTS AND REMEDIES
Spotting problems early

By arranging for your dog to visit the veterinarian on a regular basis, you can be sure that any problems will be detected at an early stage, which in turn should make treatment more straightforward.

Blockage of the anal glands

One of the commonest problems that many dogs experience are those that affect the anal glands. These are a pair of small sacs that are located just inside the anus. These sacs have an important scent-marking function, producing a pungent liquid which is transferred to the feces as they are passed out of the body. This odor enables both wild and domestic dogs to recognize each other.

Unfortunately, in domestic dogs, these sacs often become blocked, which causes them to swell up and become very uncomfortable. The dog frequently tries to relieve the irritation by so-called "scooting" — dragging its hindquarters over the carpet indoors or an area of grass outdoors. It may also try to chew and bite this part of its body. Its efforts are likely to be in vain, however, with the result that abscesses may form in the sacs, making it very painful for the dog to defecate.

Your veterinarian will be able to free the blockage and empty these sacs, although if they are not treated and the secretions form into solid plugs, it may be necessary to anesthetize the dog and flush the sacs through to break down the blockage. Recurrences can be quite common, but adding bulk to the diet, in the form of bran available from pet stores, may help to ensure that these sacs function properly in the future.

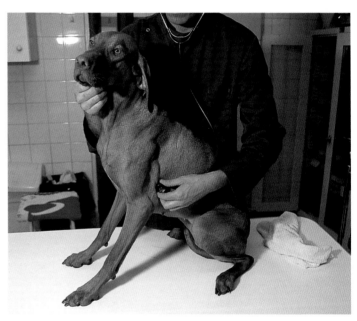

Listening to the sounds of a dog's heart will alert a veterinarian to any potential problems. Dogs can be susceptible to heart disease, especially as they become older, with some heart defects afflicting puppies.

Practical Pointer

If your dog's breath is bad, arrange for a veterinary check-up. It may simply have a bad tooth or gum disease, although, alternatively, this can be a sign of kidney failure. Once diagnosed, this condition can now be controlled largely by careful dietary manipulation, at least for a time.

Practical Pointer

The heart itself is relatively easy to locate, being found opposite the point of the elbow on the left side of the dog's body.

Heart malfunctions

More regular health checks, roughly every six months, may be recommended for older dogs. By listening to your dog's chest with a stethoscope, your veterinarian will be able to pick up any misfunctioning of the heart, which is relatively common at this stage in life. Dogs rarely suffer from coronary disease, however, unlike people, but they are more susceptible to valvular disorders.

Typical symptoms of valvular disease in dogs may be coughing and tiredness after a walk. This suggests that the mitral valve on the left side of the heart may have become thickened, and so is no longer working effectively. In contrast, when the failure involves the tricuspid valve on the right side, blood does not flow back as effectively as normal to the heart. This results in body organs, such as the liver, becoming swollen. In some cases, both valves may be affected, and the dog will then display a combination of these symptoms.

Effective treatment can be given to improve the dog's quality of life — digitalis, for example, helps to improve the contractibility of the heart muscle, making it work more effectively in spite of the valvular damage in the organ. Diuretic drugs will serve to remove excess fluid which builds up in the circulation as a result of the failing heart, so that the heart has to pump less hard, and can function more effectively. Once the initial course of drugs has been completed, the dose will have to be adapted down to a maintenance level, and continued throughout the rest of the dog's life, but this is not particularly expensive.

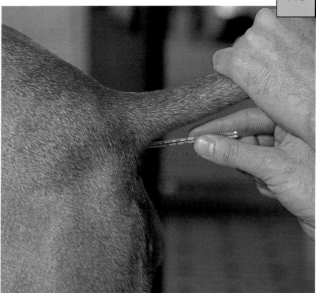

Taking a dog's temperature will help give an indication of its overall state of health. This procedure needs to be undertaken carefully however, so as not to cause pain or injury. The dog will need to be restrained for this purpose.

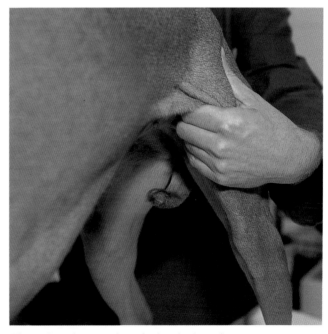

The easiest place to take a dog's pulse is as shown here, just inside the hind leg where the femoral artery runs. The pulse rate can be especially important after an injury. When trying to find your dog's pulse, do not press hard on the skin, as this tends to mask it.

Administering medicines

It is no coincidence that dogs are now living longer than ever before. This is thanks in part to a better understanding of their veterinary needs, with some practices now even holding special clinics for older dogs. In contrast, wolves and other wild dogs will be lucky to survive in the wild for as long.

Giving pills

There are a number of very basic health-care procedures which owners of domestic dogs may have to carry out on occasions, and it is much easier to practice with a puppy. Giving a pill to a dog is a fairly simple task, but is one which some owners find quite difficult. It may be possible to hide the pill in your dog's food but this is impossible if you are using a dried food diet as the pill cannot be concealed.

In any event, it is important to train your dog to allow you to open up its mouth, to take a toy away for example, if the dog refuses to drop it. Follow the technique outlined on this page *(right)* and your dog should allow you to open its mouth and give it the pill it requires. If your dog is clearly reluctant to swallow its medication try stroking the dog under the throat which should help to make it swallow.

Giving liquid medication

Giving liquid medication is relatively straight-forward as well, although it may help to lift the dog onto a bench, in a shed for example, rather than carrying out this task on the floor, where the dog will be more likely to struggle. By placing it on a bench, it should be less inclined to struggle. In the case of the larger breeds, be sure to bend your back so as not to injure yourself when lifting the dog. Place your left arm around its chest, and reach round its hind legs with your other hand, clasping the dog to your body when picking it up.

Avoid suddenly squirting the medication into the dog's mouth, as this could cause it to spit it out, or even choke. Instead, maintain a steady pressure on the syringe handle, trickling the medication into its mouth slowly. Insert the

nozzle well back in the mouth, so that the liquid can run down the throat rather than out of the sides of the mouth.

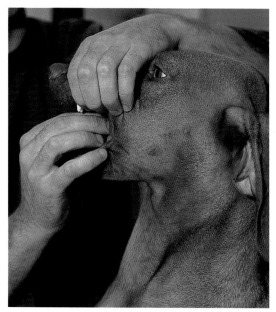

Giving your dog a pill can be carried out quite easily by placing your left hand across the nose, with your finger and thumb on each side steadying the jaws.

Use your right hand to pry down the lower jaw and slip the pill into the dog's mouth. (Reverse if you are left-handed.) Keep the jaws upright to ensure the pill falls to the back of the mouth. Keep the jaws closed to encourage the dog to swallow the pill.

Alternative health care

The growth of interest in alternative health care means there is a growing number of veterinary practices prepared to offer treatments based on herbalism or homeopathy. In the wild where dogs are reliant on their own abilities to treat themselves, they may eat coarse stems of grass for example, In order to vomit. This behavior is also often seen in domestic dogs, particularly when they are suffering from an accumulation of roundworms.

Herbalism

There is one essential difference between herbalism and homeopathy. Herbalism is more closely related to conventional medicine, but it relies entirely on plant extracts rather than on synthetic drugs. However, a number of conventional drugs were originally derived from herbs. The heart drug digitalis, for example, was originally derived from foxgloves.

Some herbal products such as raspberry-leaf tablets are recommended for preventive purposes. These are often used as a means of preventing whelping problems when a bitch is due to give birth. Seaweed powder is popular as a tonic, as it is a valuable source of iodine, which is used by the thyroid glands in the neck for the production of hormones which regulate the body's metabolism. Tea-tree extract has soothing antiseptic properties, and is valued for treating skin conditions.

Homeopathy

Homeopathy differs significantly, since its advocates believe in the principle that "like cures like". This means the treatment of a condition needs the use of a substance which will itself produce similar symptoms. The founding father of modern homeopathy was Samuel Hahnemann. Many of his treatments now in use derive from a wide range of sources, often coming from both animal and mineral origins rather than solely from plants.

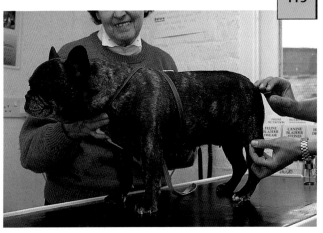

A wide variety of alternative health treatments are now being appied in the veterinary field, as here, where this French bulldog is receiving acupuncture from its veterinarian. The costs of such treatments may still be covered by veterinary insurance.

Several different homeopathic remedies may be available to treat one particular condition. There is no single treatment. Homeopathic veterinarians much prefer to concentrate on the overall signs associated with the dog's illness, rather than on any specific symptoms. This holistic approach ensures that the remedy can be tailored specifically to meet the individual's needs.

Homeopathic treatments are available in a variety of forms, including tablets, powders, and liquids, so they are as easy to administer as conventional remedies. One aspect of homeopathy stressed by its practitioners, however, is the fact that there are no side-effects. It is even possible to give dogs specific vaccines made on homeopathic principles.

Other options

Other alternative health-care options which may sometimes be applied include acupuncture, which can be especially useful for the treatment of painful injuries. Bach Flower Therapy devotees also claim that this can have a calming effect on particularly nervous dogs.

An image of Samuel Hahnemann (1755–1843) regarded as the founder of modern homeopathy.

HEALTH
Disease threats

As the number of dogs has risen significantly, especially in urban areas, so has the potential for the spread of disease. Vaccinations will help to reduce the likelihood of infections, but because outbreaks of killer diseases, such as distemper, are relatively rare, epidemics do flare up when owners forget, or simply do not bother, to have their pets vaccinated.

Stray dogs in an urban area can spread infections rapidly, with the dog's tendency to sniff leaving it exposed to infections transmitted via urine. Public places such as parks, where many dogs are exercised, can be especially dangerous for unvaccinated dogs.

Diseases can be easily spread from dog to dog by direct contact, which is why it is so important to ensure that vaccinations are kept up to date. Without this protection, dogs are at serious risk of falling ill.

Parvovirus

The age of the dog infected can have an impact on the course of the disease. Young puppies infected with parvovirus — a disease which became widespread among the world's dog population from the late 1970s onwards – are liable to suffer from heart disease as a result of the infection, while at a later stage in life, severe blood-stained diarrhea will be more common, with the corresponding damage to the intestinal lining being permanent.

Distemper, or hard pad

Other major viral diseases that dogs need to be protected against include distemper, also sometimes called hard pad. Once the virus has spread through the dog's body, typical symptoms are likely to be vomiting and diarrhea. Distemper also attacks the nervous system, where the effects are not often noticeable until many years later. A dog which suffers from occasional fits, especially if there is also some twitching of the facial muscles, is likely to have been infected by distemper early in life.

Thickening of the pads on the feet is another long-standing sign, which is why this disease is also known as hard pad. In the case of infection in young puppies, their teeth can become brownish as a result of damage to the protective coat of enamel.

Canine adenovirus

Canine adenovirus (CAV) type 1, which causes infectious hepatitis, affecting the dog's liver, is another serious disease. It is sometimes called "blue eye," because infected dogs which survive this disease often have a bluish haze over the surface of their eyes. They will remain infectious to other dogs for possibly six months, passing the virus in their urine. In contrast, CAV type 2 affects the respiratory tract, and is often implicated in cases of kennel cough (see page 125).

Leptospirosis

Another serious illness of dogs which can be prevented by vaccination is the bacterial illness known as leptospirosis. Again, there are two forms of this disease, one of which is linked to rats. Those dogs that hunt rats, such as terriers, are especially vulnerable to it. The other form is spread via dog's urine, with the result that all dogs can be at risk in the event of an outbreak.

A skin tumor on the leg of a bull terrier. In some cases, such growths may be caused by viruses and although they may be removed surgically, they will frequently recur in older individuals, whose immune system may be weakened. White dogs are especially vulnerable.

Practical Pointer

Tell your veterinarian if you suspect that your bitch is pregnant when taking her for a vaccination. This will affect the type of vaccine which can be used.

BASIC INSTINCTS • Illness in wild dogs

One of the less obvious advantages of maintaining a territory is the fact that other dogs will not be inclined to enter the area, and so the likelihood of disease being spread is correspondingly reduced. Even so, wild dogs can succumb to diseases that are associated with their prey, such as anthrax, which will wipe out wildlife (and potentially people) quite indiscriminately when an outbreak occurs in an area.

All warm-blooded animals are potentially vulnerable to the rabies virus which is spread via saliva. Dogs usually encounter the infection through being bitten. Within the pack, if one dog develops the virus, then it can be transmitted readily to the others, and will prove fatal.

Transmission of infection

Other animals apart from dogs can be infected with and transmit the rabies virus. In the United States, skunks and raccoons are the major wildlife carriers of the infection. Be especially suspicious of any wild animal which appears to be unusually friendly. It could suddenly respond by biting you, and so transmit the rabies virus.

It is not even necessary for the skin to be broken by the animal's teeth, since saliva containing the virus can enter via cuts on the hands. The length of time for symptoms to become apparent depends on the proximity of the bite to the central nervous system. The virus passes along the peripheral nervous system and

Rabies

This is the most dreaded disease that can afflict wild and domestic dogs, because it can be transmitted to humans. Once clinical signs develop, the outcome is invariably fatal. In several parts of the world, wild dogs are the main carriers of the disease, with domestic dogs being infected by a bite from an infected wild dog. In Europe, the red fox is the main carrier of rabies, while further east, in Asia, the remaining wolf population represents a major threat.

There have been major advances in the battle to control and ultimately eliminate this infection, although, at present, there are very few parts of the world which are free from rabies. These are essentially islands, such as Australia, the British Isles and Iceland. Rigorous quarantine measures are presently employed to reduce the likelihood of infection being introduced to these countries, although there are some moves to replace quarantine with a strict vaccination program.

International quarantine measures have been established to guard against the introduction of rabies to parts of the world where it does not occur in the native wildlife. Quarantine requirements vary from country to country, depending on the level of risk.

ultimately reaches the brain, at which point its deadly effects will soon become apparent.

Symptoms

Rabies is especially alarming in dogs which develop "mad dog syndrome", in which their aggression becomes uncontrollable as the virus starts to exert its deadly effects. These rabid dogs find noises exceedingly disturbing — this is frequently one of the early signs of the clinical illness. They will then start to attack almost anything with which they come into contact — including inert objects, as well as any living creatures which cross their path. In contrast to the human manifestation of the disease, however, rabid dogs do not develop hydrophobia, or fear of water.

However, the paralytic form of the disease can be more dangerous as far as dog-owners are concerned. One of the earliest signs is a drooping of the lower jaw, which gives the dog the appearance of having an object stuck in its mouth. Examining the mouth at this stage is exceedingly dangerous, because of the risk of coming into contact with the virus. The dog will not usually attempt to bite — instead, the paralysis will spread through its body, resulting in its demise within hours of the initial signs becoming apparent.

A pack of grey wolves have long inspired fear among people, but they are not usually aggressive toward people. Most wolf attacks on humans can be linked to rabid animals which have lost their natural sense of caution, and they will then attack their victim in a frenzy.

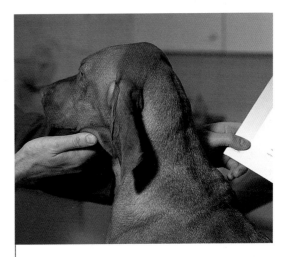

Practical Pointer

Vaccination for rabies is compulsory in many parts of the world where the virus is present, but the regulations do differ from country to country. Your veterinarian will be able to advise you accordingly.

External parasites

Both wild and domestic dogs are at risk from external parasites, which comprise various mites, lice, fleas, and ticks. In the case of wild dogs, such as foxes, the effects can be so debilitating that the animals move burrows to escape the worst of the infection. In animals already weakened by a lack of food, these parasitic infections, particularly mange, can ultimately prove to be fatal.

BASIC INSTINCTS • Under threat
Parasites can gain a hold on a weakened individual, and finally lead to its demise. Most wild dogs actually live for a much shorter period of time than their domestic relatives, because of the dangers and potential food shortages which they inevitably have to face in these surroundings.

The main external parasites

If you notice that your dog is scratching a lot, check it for signs of parasitic infestation.

FLEAS

Domestic dogs are most likely to suffer from fleas. These parasites have become a year-round problem in temperate areas, now that many more homes are equipped with central heating, although they are still most prevalent in the summer.

Repeated scratching and itching, with the dog even chewing its skin on occasions, are the common indicators of

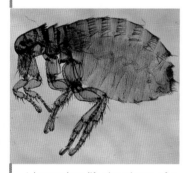

A larger than life-size picture of a flea, a parasite that can cause a dog much discomfort.

the presence of fleas. A special flea comb should be used, which will confirm the presence of these parasites. Groom the dog outdoors, so that any fleas which jump off will be less likely to cause problems. You are most likely to see tiny blackish specks among the fur, which are the droppings of the fleas. These contain traces of undigested blood sucked out from the dog's skin, and will leave reddish deposits if moistened on damp,

white blotting paper. There are various ways of combating fleas. In the short term, a powder or spray is the best way of killing them. Special grooming combs with hollow teeth can be used to dispense flea powder deep within the fur, where it is less likely to be shaken out.

In severe cases, you may be advised to bathe your dog using a special medicated wash, which should be very effective in destroying the fleas in its coat. But this alone will not be enough — eggs laid on the dog by adult fleas will drop off, usually in or near the dog's bedding, and rapidly hatch into larvae. These pupate, and emerge as adult fleas leaping onto the dog when it is in range again.

It is therefore essential to wash all bedding thoroughly, and to vacuum in the vicinity of the dog's bed, particularly close to the walls, in order to reduce the likelihood of reinfection. There are now treatments, based on insect growth-regulators, that prevent the development of fleas or render them sterile. These are useful for preventing any build-up of these parasites, which may bite people as well, although they will not live on our bodies.

TICKS

Ticks are far less of a problem on dogs, although they may be a nuisance, particularly if your dog is exercised on heathland. The tick will anchor itself onto the dog's skin with its strong mouthparts, and soon swells in size as it sucks the dog's body

This magnified picture of a tick shows it sticking closely to the dog's hair.

fluids. Do not pull off the parasite, because it could leave its head in the skin, creating an infection. Instead, smear its body with petroleum jelly, which will block its breathing holes, causing it to detach itself. Ticks can be carriers of Lyme disease, a serious illness causing fever and affecting the joints, as well as blood-borne, parasitic ailments.

LICE

Lice are rarely a problem with dogs, although they can sometimes be encountered in puppies reared under poor conditions. They stick to the hair, where their egg cases, called nits, will also be seen. An antiflea treatment will kill lice.

MANGE

Mange, caused by microscopic mites is a problem to treat. The two types are demodectic and sarcoptic mange. *Demodex* mites are often associated with dachshund breeds, and live deep within the hair follicles, making treatment difficult. *Sarcoptes* mites are more superficial, and cause reddening of the bare skin on the underside of the thighs. Skin scrapings may be necessary to confirm the cause of the problem.

Internal parasites

The diet of carnivores such as dogs can leave them exposed to internal parasites, whose life cycles are closely linked with their prey. This link has largely been broken in the case of the domestic dog, however, which is fed in many cases on prepared foods, free from parasites, rather than on raw fish or meat. Even so, they can suffer badly from roundworms, which are transmitted directly from one dog to another.

Practical Pointer

Follow the deworming program as recommended by your veterinarian carefully, in order to prevent the likelihood of a build-up of these parasites.

Some parasites, notably tapeworms, may have a two stage or indirect life-cycle, which means they must pass through an intermediate host such as a flea or sheep before being able to infect a dog again.

The main internal parasites

As well as having serious effects on your dog, worms can also have quite serious effects on humans.

ROUNDWORM

Puppies may even be born with roundworms, the result of an infection which they received from their mother before birth. The particular worry about the roundworm known as *Toxocara canis* arises from the fact that it can also infect people, particularly young children. The risk is greatest in places such as public parks, where dogs are frequently exercised, although such parasites can be equally deposited by foxes, or even wolves in some areas.

The key to curbing a roundworm risk is deworming, particularly of bitches prior to pregnancy. This will serve to minimize the risk of infection in the newly born puppies. The bitch may also infect her offspring directly after birth, by transferring larval worms to them in her milk. Once the worms have matured in the intestinal tract, the puppies themselves will then produce microscopic *Toxocara* eggs in their feces.

Children must always be taught to wash their hands after playing with a puppy, and always before eating, so that they do not ingest these eggs. Otherwise there is a minute risk of the larvae migrating around their body to the eye, where it could cause a cyst and, ultimately, blindness.

TAPEWORMS

Tapeworms can be quite easily distinguished from roundworms by their flattened shape. Dogs can be affected by a number of different types. One of the commonest forms is the dog tapeworm, *Dipylidium caninum*. It has a life cycle which involves the flea, so it is advisable to treat dogs which have had a problem with fleas with a tapeworm remedy afterward.

The tapeworm eggs pass out of the anus, and stick to the fur, where they are ingested by fleas. If the dog then catches and swallows a parasitized flea, the tapeworm is likely to develop in its body. Tablets are the usual treatment for tapeworms.

HEARTWORM

Depending on where you live in the world, other internal parasites may be of some concern, especially heartworm (*Dirofilaria immitis*), which is a potential problem in warmer countries. Biting insects, such as mosquitoes, spread the infection when they feed, by injecting the so-called *microfilariae* into the dog's body. These immature worms then develop in the circulatory system, localizing ultimately in the vicinity of the heart, with potentially dire consequences. Preventive treatment, which entails giving regular medication, is therefore advisable.

HOOKWORMS

Hookworms can also have serious effects. These parasites tend to be found in damp surroundings, again often in warmer parts of the world. They are able to bore directly into the feet of dogs and other animals. They may then migrate to the intestines. Depending on the species of hookwork concerned they may cause severe anemia. Hookworms actually contributed directly to the decline of the red wolf in its last remaining stronghold (Texas), before the present reintroduction program was undertaken.

Practical Pointer

Clear up thoroughly after your dog, using a suitable tool. This will reduce the likelihood of adding to any existing contamination of the ground with *Toxocara* eggs, either at home or in public places. Eggs are not immediately infective. They take several days to mature outside the body, but can survive for years.

BOARDING KENNELS
Vacation and quarantine boarding

There are likely to be times when you may need to use the services of a boarding kennel for your dog. If you do not know the kennels in your area, ask dog-owning friends for their advice, or arrange to visit several kennels to see the facilities on offer, before confirming a booking. Those in your area can be found in the telephone book.

Choosing and booking kennels

The kennels should be clean, with secure runs and heated sleeping quarters if the weather is likely to be cold. Do not be influenced just by the premises — the attitude of the staff is also important, to ensure that your dog settles well into strange surroundings. Ask what you should bring with you. A familiar blanket, containing the scent of home, may provide reassurance for your pet during your absence, as may a toy.

You should also leave details of your veterinarian, so that the kennels will be able to contact the practice in the event of any emergency. It will also help if you can give them a contact number where you can be reached while you are away. Be sure to discuss any particular requirements of your dog in advance as well, and if you have a bitch which could come into season while you are likely to be away, arrange with your veterinarian to

Always check out boarding kennels in advance if you have not used them for your pet before. Cleanliness is obviously very important, and particular attention must be paid to the space available for exercise, so your dog does not become bored in its surroundings.

postpone this heat by means of an injection. Having a bitch on heat is likely to be especially disrupting within the confines of a kennels housing many dogs.

How will your dog settle into kennels?

Most dogs will actually settle very rapidly into such surroundings, although the change in environment can be stressful. Sharing the same air space with other dogs means that the risk of infections spreading is much higher than at home. This is why responsible kennels will always insist that all the dogs brought to them must have been currently vaccinated, and you will need to take a certificate to this effect with you when you check in your dog for its stay there.

Dogs will often bark for long periods in kennels, because of the sounds of other dogs around them. The close proximity to other dogs means that respiratory illnesses can spread easily, which is why it may be worthwhile having your pet vaccinated for kennel cough before you go away, although this is not compulsory at all kennels.

Kennel cough

There is no single cause of kennel cough but canine adenovirus type 2 and a bacterium, *Bordetella bronchoseptica*, are often involved.

Practical Pointer
Should you be unable to find your pet's vaccination certificate, your veterinarian may well be prepared to issue you with a duplicate from the practice records, although you may have to pay a fee for the extra paperwork.

Practical Pointer
Show dogs are regularly vaccinated against kennel cough. The spread of this infection is virtually impossible to prevent in areas where dogs are being brought together and housed indoors.

The vaccine will therefore not cover all the causes, but it will give a high degree of protection. This is especially valuable for older dogs, which are more likely to succumb to the infection. In most cases, an affected dog develops a distinctive cough which can be triggered easily if you place your hand on the underside of the throat. It should clear up spontaneously within about three weeks of the infection first becoming apparent, but in older individuals, it can develop into pneumonia.

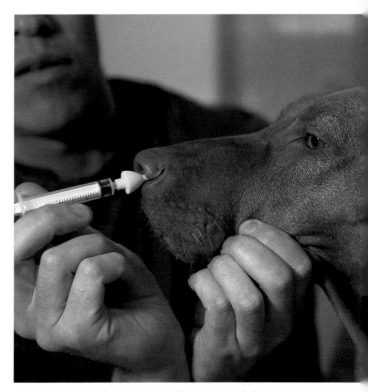

Prior to going into kennels, it may be recommended that your dog is protected against kennel cough. This vaccine is administered by being squirted up the nasal passage as shown.

BREEDING PROBLEMS
Pseudopregnancies

Wild dogs, such as wolves, have only one period of heat during the year, and within the pack it is usually only the dominant female which becomes pregnant. Even so, the other females in the pack usually become involved in rearing her young and become "pseudopregnant," which means that they have milk available. Thus, should any disaster befall the breeding female, her cubs can still be reared successfully by other pack members — otherwise they would inevitably die.

Pseudopregnancies may recur throughout the bitch's life if the animal is not neutered.

Practical Pointer

Do not feel inclined to allow a bitch to have a litter of puppies at her next heat, as this will not prevent pseudopregnancies at subsequent heats. You will also face the additional problem of finding good homes for the puppies, which can be difficult, and if you have to keep some of them yourself, will also be costly.

Pseudopregnancy in dogs

The situation in the case of the bitch, however, is slightly different. Pseudopregnancy, also known as phantom pregnancy, arises when the hormones in the bitch's body tell her that she is pregnant, although she has not actually mated. It occurs because, at the points where her eggs leave the ovary, structures called corpora lutea form. These are vital for a successful pregnancy, releasing the hormone called progesterone.

This normally allows the developing eggs to implant in the bitch's uterus, where they start developing into puppies. If mating has not actually taken place, these corpora lutea soon cease to produce this hormone, and so the signs of pregnancy do not usually become apparent.

Where the case of a pseudopregnancy is concerned, however, the output of the hormone progesterone continues. This has widespread effects on the body, creating the impression that the bitch is really pregnant. Her uterus grows in size, causing her abdomen to enlarge as a result. The output of progesterone may even be sufficient to cause the bitch's mammary glands to swell and she may actually start to produce milk.

Treatment of pseudopregnancy

A bitch suffering from a pseudopregnancy is liable to regard toys or other objects, such as shoes, as her puppies, and will be very protective toward them, snapping fiercely if you try to take them away from her. Your veterinarian will prescribe medication, possibly in the form of tranquilizers, and also hormonal treatment, which should help her over this period quite quickly, and will also dry up any milk. Otherwise, if it is left unchecked, the progesterone output can continue for up to three months in total.

Once the symptoms disappear, they are very unlikely to resurface until after the next heat, but it is often better to have the bitch neutered beforehand. This is partly because pseudopregnancies tend to recur at each season, and also because the effects often become more severe. It is also possible that bitches which suffer from pseudopregnancies could be at greater risk of developing an infection of the uterus, called pyometra, in the future. This can be potentially life threatening.

Practical Pointer

If your bitch starts to drink considerably more, this may be an early indication of a pyometra. Seek veterinary advice without delay. There may be a discharge from her vagina, but in other cases — a closed pyometra — the pus simply accumulates in the uterus.

BASIC INSTINCTS • Pack support

Death of the cubs could, in time, affect the hunting ability of the pack as a whole, causing its break-up. This applies particularly in some parts of the wolf's range, such as the far north, where large and potentially dangerous animals, such as moose, have to be overpowered by the wolves. A small pack is less likely to be able to obtain sufficient food, while the individual members run a greater risk of being killed or injured when hunting such quarry. There is real strength in numbers in this case, with pseudopregnancy providing useful support !

GROOMING &

CARE

The amount of grooming care required will depend very much on your choice of dog. Grey wolves have coats of variable length, depending largely on their area of origin. Those from the cold north tend to have longer coats than those occurring further south. Selective breeding has led to an increase in the coat length of many breeds, and if you opt for a long-haired dog of any type, you will need to be prepared to groom your pet on a daily basis. Greater emphasis on grooming is particularly important when the dog is molting. Otherwise, its coat is likely to become knotted, and the matted areas of fur will have to cut away.

Different breeds require different levels of care to their ears and eyes as well as to their teeth and nails. For example, Pekingese with their prominent eyes are quite vulnerable to problems and injuries to their eyes.

GROOMING
Brushing, washing and shampooing

Regular grooming to remove the loose hairs in your dog's coat will not only make it feel more comfortable, but should also ensure that there are less hairs shed around the home. The amount of hair shed tends to increase during spring, particularly in the case of those breeds, such as the German shepherd dog, which have dense winter coats. These are then replaced with less profuse coats for the warmer part of the year. The second major period of molting takes place in the fall, to complete the molting cycle.

There is not necessarily any need to throw away your dog's molted hair. Some owners collect it so that they can spin it and ultimately make small garments from it. The amount of grooming needed will depend on the breed concerned, with long-haired dogs, such as the Afghan hound, requiring more grooming than the sleek-coated pharaoh hound.

A variety of suitable tools may be purchased for grooming purposes. They range from simple brushes and combs to grooming mitts, which are rather like a glove and can be used to give a good gloss to the coat of sleek-coated breeds. Regular daily grooming is essential in the case of long-haired dogs, otherwise their

Practical Pointer
A recent grooming advance in the battle against fleas is a special comb that gives off a low electrical charge when operating. This will knock out any flea with which it comes into contact, and the motor cuts out to alert you to this fact. You can then locate and remove the flea easily without having to resort to chemical methods of control.

Removing loose hair from the coat with a special grooming tool will prevent its accumulating on carpeting around the home, with daily grooming being recommended. Hair will be shed almost constantly, but in greater quantities when the dog is molting in the spring particularly, losing its thicker winter coat.

hair is likely to become matted. It will then be impossible to break down these chunks of fur, so they will have to be cut out which will spoil the dog's appearance until the fur in these areas has regrown.

Inspecting the coat

Regular grooming also gives you the opportunity to check on the condition of your dog's coat, and to check on any problems, such as fleas, which may be lurking there, although to trap these parasites, you will need to use a special, fine-toothed flea comb.

Always keep a close watch for the appearance of any bald areas on your pet's coat, particularly if it has been near any farms. Hair loss in a characteristically circular pattern is the main indicator of ringworm, which, in spite of its name, is caused by a fungus rather than a parasite. This is a particular problem in young cattle, and the spores will remain in an area for a long time, on fence posts for example, where the cattle have rubbed themselves.

Once ringworm has been diagnosed, specific antifungal treatment will be required, and the grooming equipment will have to be disposed of or disinfected, because the spores can linger on it and will reinfect the dog. The main danger, however, is that members of the household could also acquire this infection. In people, it gives rise to reddish circular patches, often on exposed parts of the skin, such as the forearms. Seek medical advice if you suspect that you may have contracted this disease.

BASIC INSTINCTS • Thick coats

As with wolves, it is no coincidence that dog breeds which originated in areas where the weather is cold in the winter tend to have more profuse coats than those found further south, in the Mediterranean region, for example. The insulating down hairs close to the body help to trap warm air close to the skin, providing an insulating barrier against the cold. The actual markings of the dog will be consistent through-out its life, irrespective of when it molts.

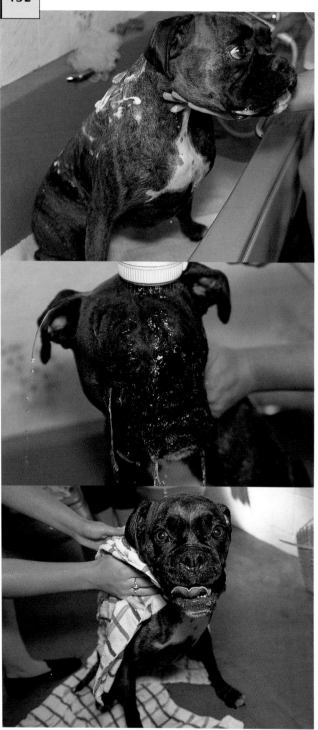

Dogs may become frightened by being placed in a bath, so it is a good idea to accustom them to this experience from an early age. Always wet the head last, as this is the part which often proves to be most distressing for them, and then rinse the shampoo out of the coat thoroughly.

Washing your dog

Most dogs will enter water readily, and they can swim if necessary, using their legs to provide the propulsive thrust under the water, while their tail serves to act as a rudder. As domestication has proceeded, so some dogs have been developed for retrieving game in marshland areas, and similar localities where swimming may be necessary. Such dogs have a dense, water-resistant coat, and they may also have webbed toes, to give greater power when swimming.

Where to wash your dog

When it comes to bathing, most dogs will benefit from a bath every three months or so, to remove any trace of that distinctive doggy odor which can linger in the home or coat, particularly if your pet has been outdoors and ended up slightly damp. It is not a good idea to use your own bath when washing your pet, first because this is not very hygienic, and second because there is also the distinct likelihood that the dog will scratch and damage the base of the bath with its claws.

It is much better to wash your dog outdoors on a fine day. If you have a small dog, you can use a suitable baby-bath as a container. In the case of a much larger animal, you will need to rely on a basic shower attachment which, for example, can be easily fitted onto the kitchen faucets and run out of a convenient window.

Special shampoos for dogs are available from pet stores. You will also need a jug, so that you can bale water over your dog. Start by filling the bath with tepid water and then lift the dog into it. Most dogs will stand quite

Practical Pointer

Do not forget to clean the underside of your dog's ear flaps when giving it a bath, but be sure that water does not run down the ear canal, while you are doing this.

Practical Pointer

For the first few days after its bath, keep your dog away from areas where cattle may have grazed recently. This is because, when deprived of their natural scent, some dogs will run off and roll in manure to regain a distinctive body odor.

happily in a bath with a non-slippery base, provided that the water is reasonably shallow and does not extend above chest level.

How to wash your dog

Using the jug, gently pour the water over the dog's hindquarters first, to wet the fur, and then apply the shampoo to create a good lather. Leave the head until last as washing this particular area is most likely to upset your pet. Take particular care to avoid any shampoo entering the dog's eyes. It may be best to use an old cloth when cleaning here.

After washing the coat thoroughly, you can then rinse out the shampoo. This is when the shower attachment, or even a garden hose, can be very useful, but you should aim to use tepid water for this purpose. Finally, lift the dog out of the bath or allow it to jump out on its own. Once out of the water, your dog will almost certainly shake itself vigorously to remove the remaining water from its coat, so stand back for a moment. You can then start to dry the dog with a large towel.

Do not allow your dog to stay outside while its coat is still wet, especially when the weather is cold, as deprived of the natural insulation of its coat, the dog is likely to catch a chill. Indoors, a hairdryer can be used to speed the drying process, provided that the noise does not disturb your pet. You should also check that it is on a relatively low heat setting, to avoid any risk of burning the dog.

Dogs will regularly clean their own coats by licking them. This is fine, but if your pet has any potentially harmful substances on its coat, such as oil, the affected area must be cleaned immediately, to prevent the contaminant being ingested.

Professional grooming

There are a number of breeds which do not molt their coats in a regular fashion. These include various terriers, such as the Bedlington, as well as the poodle breeds. If these dogs are not being kept for show purposes, their coats will require clipping every six weeks or so. Wire-coated dogs also require more grooming than usual, and need to have the dead hair stripped out of their coats in the spring and autumn. Professional grooming parlors will undertake these tasks for you, and will even bathe your pet if required.

When choosing where to take your dog to be groomed, you can seek recommendations from the breeder who supplied your pet, or your veterinarian may also feel able to advise you. Alternatively, you can simply resort to the telephone book, but bear in mind

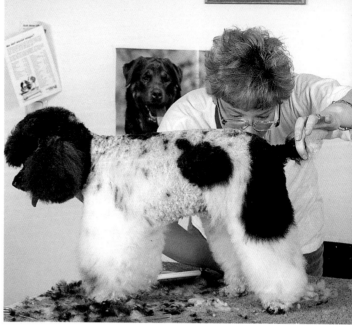

Some dogs react better to being groomed in strange surroundings, where they will be less inclined to treat the procedure as a game. It is important to position the dog at a comfortable height and in a good light.

that dog-groomers are rather like hairdressers — not all are necessarily equally talented or as well trained, so it can be reassuring to go to someone with qualifications in this field.

Poodles

Although not everyone likes the appearance of breeds such as poodles, with their highly manicured coats, it is often forgotten that the appearance of these dogs today is actually a direct reflection of their working ancestry. They were formerly used as retrievers of waterfowl and so were often required to swim in what could frequently be very cold water.

While a thick, heavy coat would protect the dog against the cold, it would also tend to drag it down when soaked. A compromise was therefore reached whereby the fur on the muscular parts of the body was trimmed short, while the joints were left with a good covering of fur to protect the dog when it was in water close to freezing.

There are some breeds, such as poodles, which are best groomed professionally. For poodles there are various types of trim, depending on whether you intend to show your dog or not.

These two photographs reveal just how the appearance of this golden retriever has been improved by bathing and grooming. Having been bathed however, beware that your dog does not go off and roll in the dirt to enhance its scent. Bathing every two months or so is usually recommended to curb the characteristic "doggy" odor.

There are a number of different grooming styles available for poodles today. Puppies are traditionally given the so-called "lamb clip," in which the coat is trimmed to an even length over the entire head and body. This is the simplest style, and there is no reason why adult dogs being kept as pets cannot have their coats kept in this fashion.

Much more elaborate and costly is the so-called "lion clip," which is the style often favored for show purposes. Not surprisingly, a number of breeders and exhibitors are also groomers, having learnt the craft so they can groom their own dogs effectively.

Practical Pointer

You can find out about dog-grooming courses through advertisements in the dog press, or your local library may be able to advise you.

A selection of grooming tools that can be purchased from most pet stores.

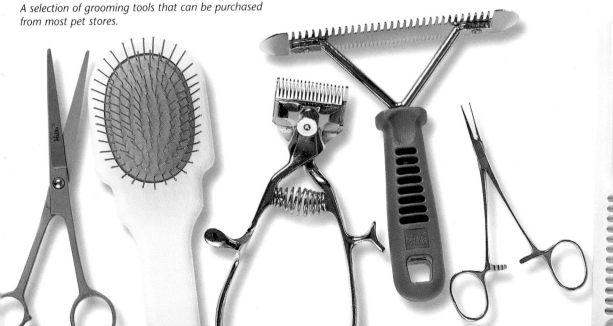

Dogs appreciate the comfort of having their own bed for sleeping purposes, which should be lined with a blanket which can be washed as necessary.

Dogs outdoors

Dogs are relatively hardy, although clearly those without a body covering of fur will be most susceptible to the weather. When a dog goes out for a walk on a wet day, you may want to equip it with a jacket, especially if the weather is also cold. Apart from breeds such as the Mexican hairless, a number of other breeds are likely to feel the cold more than others.

Weather protection

These include greyhounds and whippets, which have little insulating body fat beneath the skin, and a relatively thin, short covering of hair. Elderly dogs will also benefit from the protection of a jacket when the weather is bad. The distance from the back of the neck to the base of the tail is the significant measurement when choosing a dog jacket.

The actual design is not necessarily important, but check the way in which the jacket is tied around the dog's body. This should be by means of a secure tie that is actually attached to the jacket, rather than simply looping around it. Otherwise the jacket can be more easily lost when the dog is out walking, by getting caught up on undergrowth and being pulled off as your pet struggles to free itself.

A button is a far less reliable means of attachment than a buckle.

Dealing with a muddy dog

When exercising your dog, it is inevitable, especially if you are walking off the grass in woodland, that your dog will end up with muddy paws. The mud may often extend up the legs as well, particularly in the case of breeds such as setters, which have longer hair, described as feathering, at the back of their legs.

It is useful to keep an old towel in the car with which you can dry your dog's feet before allowing it back into the vehicle. Removing mud from the legs is difficult, however, apart from by washing the dog, which should not be carried out too often. The best solution is to wait until the mud dries, when it can be groomed out of the coat easily with a brush.

Foot problems

Other, more serious grooming problems may arise following a walk, particularly in the late summer. Always check your dog's feet at the end of the walk, particularly in the case of a long-haired breed, for any signs of grass seeds sticking to the coat, or between the pads.

Clothing for dogs now extends well beyond a simple coat, and can be used to protect most of the body from becoming muddy. This will also serve to keep a dog warm after it has been in water.

If left, especially under the feet, the sharp end of the seed may penetrate the skin between the pads and work its way into the foot as the dog walks. Grass seeds can move up the legs, and cause great pain and discomfort.

A frequent early indication is when the dog repeatedly chews and nibbles at a foot, and is reluctant to place its weight on it. This apparent lameness helps to distinguish between the likely presence of a grass seed and an infestation of harvest mite (*Trombicula autumnalis*) in the foot. The free-living form of this parasite resembles a tiny red spider, and the larvae themselves congregate on the underside of the foot, causing a severe irritation between the toes.

A beach can pose a number of hazards for dogs if they are left to roam here unsupervised. This dog became immersed in wet mud, and might have become trapped. It will now need to be bathed and groomed.

BASIC INSTINCTS • Sleeping out

Dogs are generally hardy, with wolves and foxes being found in areas of the world where the temperature regularly falls below freezing. Their dense coats help to conserve body heat, along with their habit of curling into a ball, as shown by this red fox. As they become warmer, so they will stretch out and lie on their side.

CARE

Dogs show considerable variation in the appearance of their eyes and ears. In some breeds, such as the Pekingese, the eyes have become especially prominent, while in the case of the basset hound, the ear flaps, compared with those of wolves, have become greatly enlarged and are no longer held vertically.

The bloodhound makes an affectionate companion and is good with children. It needs a lot of regular exercise and is best suited to a rural environment. The bloodhound should be groomed daily.

Care of the ears

It is thought that many hounds have pendulous ears to protect the inner ear canal from being damaged by vegetation as they move through undergrowth. Pendulous ears, however, have the potential to favor the development of infections, especially when they are heavy and covered in long hair. Spaniels often suffer from ear infections, which can be caused by a combination of various bacteria, fungi and ear mites. This is why it is important for the ears to be examined by your veterinarian, so that the most appropriate treatment can be given.

Ear cleaning should always be carried out gently and carefully using soft absorbent cotton lightly dipped in hand warm water. For any other treatment, consult your veterinarian and follow his or her instructions.

Unfortunately, relapses are not uncommon, and before long, your dog may be pawing at its ears again, in obvious pain. Early treatment will give the greatest likelihood of success and you should follow the instructions for the use of the medication carefully, in the hope that the problem will not recur.

Be sure to finish the course of treatment — some owners do not bother once their pet appears to have recovered, and this can lead to a rapid recurrence of the problem. In the worst cases, where there has been a chronic inflammation in the ears for a long period of time, the only solution will be surgery. Known as an aural resection, this entails opening the ear canal so that it can be properly cleaned and will subsequently remain open. This causes the dog no apparent discomfort once the wound has healed. Nor is it very disfiguring, because, in the case of breeds with pendulous ears, it is generally hidden by the ear flap.

Care of the eyes

Dogs with prominent eyes are most vulnerable to eye injury, while their shortened face makes them prone to tear-staining, because of the compression of the nasolachrymal glands on

EARS

BUTTON
The ear flap folding forward and the tip lying close to the skull, covering the orifice and pointing toward the eye *(Irish terrier)*.

HOUND
Triangular and rounded, the ear flap falling forward and lying close to the head *(Beagle)*.

PRICKED
Standing erect and generally pointed at the tips *(German shepherd dog)*.

ROSE
A small drop ear that folds over and back so as to reveal the burr *(Pug)*.

the lower eyelid. The accumulation of dirt around the lower part of the eye should be gently bathed with some absorbent cotton as necessary, to wipe away the tear-staining.

If the eyes need to be treated with drops, be sure to hold your dog's head securely so that it cannot twist away, causing the drops of medication to miss their target. If this does happen, or your dog blinks at the vital moment, you will need to repeat the treatment.

In order to maintain a therapeutic dose of the drug, you may have to treat an infected eye about four times a day. This is because, unfortunately, the fluid in the eye will wash it away, diluting its effectiveness. However, eye ailments can respond very rapidly to treatment.

If you are prescribed ointment to treat your dog's eyes, squeeze this out gently from the bottom of the tube, applying it in a horizontal line across the eye if possible. Again, as with all medication, it is important to complete the treatment, even if your dog appears to have recovered fully beforehand.

Wipe away any tear-staining using absorbent cotton dampened with a little water. Use gentle strokes away from the eyes until the staining is removed.

EYES

GLOBULAR
Appearing to protrude, but in fact not bulging when viewed in profile *(Chihuahua)*.

ALMOND
Almond-shaped *(German shepherd dog)*.

HAW
The term used for the third membrane in the inside of the eye. Its appearance is a fault in some breeds *(Bloodhound)*.

CIRCULAR
As round as possible *(Smooth-haired fox terrier)*.

Teeth and claws

Domestic dogs, which tend to enjoy a more leisured life style today compared with their ancestors, are more vulnerable to dental disease, as well as to overgrown claws. Too many treats and soft food, and less time spent gnawing on bones, have left dogs' teeth more vulnerable at a time when they are living longer than ever before. Meanwhile, lack of exercise has ensured that the claws do not receive as much wear as they would in the wild.

Care of the teeth

Having accustomed your puppy to having its mouth opened on a regular basis, you can start to brush its teeth every week or so. This will help to prevent the accumulation of plaque, which is likely to lead on to gum disease and weaken the roots of the teeth. Special toothbrushes and paste are available for cleaning dogs' teeth. Ordinary toothpaste is not suitable — dogs dislike its taste. Do not brush the teeth hard, or cause the gums to bleed, but remember it is at the junction between the teeth and the gums where problems are most likely to arise.

It is also possible to help the teeth to stay in good condition by providing chews and offering your dog dried food on occasions. Dogs' teeth do not develop dental cavities like ours. If necessary, your veterinarian will clean your dog's teeth under anesthetic, removing any heavy accumulations of tartar. Bad breath, coupled with a tendency to dribble, are typical indicators of serious dental disease in dogs.

Clipping the claws

A dog's dew claws are the claws which are most likely to become overgrown, simply because they are not in contact with the ground and will continue growing. If they were not removed early in life, they will need to be trimmed back,

Practical Pointer

A long-haired dog which dribbles because of bad teeth may be suffering from an infection of the outer lips. Trimming back the hair around the mouth may be advisable under these circumstances.

Dental care begun early in life should help to save your dog from discomfort with its teeth when it is older. There are special toothbrush and paste kits which you can obtain for dogs, and if used regularly, they should help to prevent a build up of tartar which is likely to be very damaging.

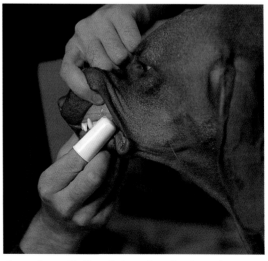

Some dogs will allow their teeth to be cleaned more directly with a finger brush. This can be especially useful to prevent accumulations of food and tartar building up at the margin of the gums and teeth.

before they can curve around into the pad behind. Alternatively, it is possible to remove the dew claws but this is a more major operation in an older dog.

When it comes to clipping these or other claws, you can either arrange for your veterinarian to undertake this task, or do it yourself. For this purpose, you will need a suitably stout pair of clippers, which can be obtained from most pet stores. Choose those of the guillotine type, with a sliding blade, as they are easier to use with precision, and you are less likely to cut the claws too short and cause them to bleed.

Start by placing the dog at a convenient height, on a table or bench in a good light, so that you can have a clear view of the claws. You should start by locating the blood supply, which extends a short distance down each claw as a pinkish streak. It is then a matter of cutting the claw some distance below the point where this streak disappears.

The claws of some dogs are blackish, which can make it extremely difficult to determine the extent of the blood supply. Under these circumstances, cutting needs to be carried out with some caution, and it may actually be advisable to seek veterinary advice rather than risk hurting your pet.

Gauging accurately where the cut should be made is largely a matter of experience. If you do have the misfortune to clip a claw too short, pressing on the cut end for a few moments with damp absorbent cotton should stimulate the clotting process. Applying a styptic pencil, as used for shaving nicks, may also be helpful.

Most dogs do not resent having their nails clipped, although it helps if they have been

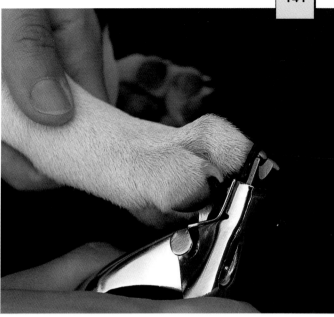

Puppies in particular often have sharp tips to their claws, and it can be helpful to trim the ends off with special clippers, to prevent any risk of the dog becoming caught up on bedding. Always check for the blood supply first, to prevent any bleeding.

trained since puppyhood to be accustomed to having their feet picked up. Although nail-clipping itself should be painless if carried out correctly, some dogs dislike being restrained for this purpose. When clipping the front claws, it may help if someone else picks up and holds the dog. You will then be able to reach these claws easily, and the dog will be less inclined to struggle under these circumstances because he or she will feel secure and will not be so afraid of falling.

These guillotine-type clippers provide a simple and safe means of trimming claws.

Practical Pointer

Never be tempted to use scissors to try to cut a dog's claws. They are unlikely to be strong enough to cut though the nail cleanly, and may well cause it to split.

INDEX

CREDITS

Quarto would like to acknowledge and thank the following for providing pictures used in this book. While every effort has been made to acknowledge copyright holders we would like to apologize should there have been any omissions.

Key: t=top b=below c=center
         l=left   r=right

David Alderton p.117(b); **Animal Photography** p.1(b), p.25, p.28(b), p.30, p.33, p.36(t), p.37, p.44, p.46, p.47, p.51(b), p.53(t), p.54(b), p.56, p.59(t), p.64, p.69(b), p.77, p.79(l), p.80(t), p.84(t), p.90, p.91(r), p.93, p.95(l), p.96(t), p.99(b), p.101(r), p.115(t), p.118(b), p.122, p.128, p.135(t&c), p.136(tl), p.138(t); **Ann Ronan at Image Select** p.20, p.22, p.51(t), p.52(t), p.115(b); **Ardea** p.126, p.133; **ET Archive** p.16, p.17; **Marc Henrie** p.60(t), p.74, p.81(t); Jacana p.1(t), p.2, p.3, p.6,

p.7, p.19(t), p.31, p.34, p.35(c&b), p.43(t), p.49, p.57, p.62, p.65, p.69(t), p.71(t&b), p.76, p.81(b), p.86, p.87, p.92(b), p.94, p.95(r), p.96(b), p.98(l&r), p.99(t), p.106, p.107, p.108, p.111, p.119(t), p.121(t&b), p.124, p.127, p.131, p.134(t), p.136(b); **Monty Sloan/Wolf Park** p.43(b), p.91(l); **Papilio** p.15; **Shoot Photographic** p.83, p.110(t), p.116(b), **The Streatham Hill Veterinary Surgery** p.104; **Bruce Tanner Photographer** p.26(t), p.42, p.55(b), p.60(b), p.88(t), p.89(t), p.105(t&b), p.117(t), p.118(t), p.120, p.129, p.137(b); **Warren Photographic** p.14, p.24(t), p.28(t), p.61(t), p.66, p.68, p.70, p.75(t), p.84(b), p.102(t); **Windrush** p.73, p.78, p.137(t).

All other photographs are copyright of Quarto Publishing plc.

Quarto would like to thank the following for supplying props and equipment for photography:
Cally Pet Stores
345a Caledonian Rd
London N1 1DW

Petsmart House
Dorcan Complex
Faraday Road
Swindon
SN3 5HQ

We would also like to thank the following for their help with this project:
Wolf Park
Battle Ground
Indiana 47920
USA
The Streatham Hill Veterinary Surgery
101 Sternhold Avenue
Streatham Hill
London SW2